Unit Resource Guide
Unit 20

Connections:
An Assessment Unit

THIRD EDITION

KENDALL/HUNT PUBLISHING COMPANY
4050 Westmark Drive   Dubuque, Iowa 52002

A TIMS® Curriculum
University of Illinois at Chicago

UIC The University of Illinois
at Chicago

The original edition was based on work supported by the National Science Foundation under grant No. MDR 9050226 and the University of Illinois at Chicago. Any opinions, findings, and conclusions or recommendations expressed in this publication are those of the author(s) and do not necessarily reflect the views of the granting agencies.

Printed in the United States of America

1 2 3 4 5 6 7 8 9 10   11 10 09 08 07

Letter Home

Connections: An Assessment Unit

Date: _____

Dear Family Member:

At this time of year it is appropriate to look back and assess students' progress in mathematics. The activities in this last unit review and assess the concepts and skills we have worked on throughout the year. Two of the assessments are similar to activities and labs students have done during the year and two are traditional tests. We also review and complete our portfolios.

In this unit, we investigate the relationship between the height of a tower of connecting cubes and its volume. Using this information, we should be able to tell the volume of a tower given its height or vice versa. As your son or daughter works on the lab and other activities, he or she is assessed not only for understanding the math content, but also for his or her abilities to solve problems and communicate results and solutions.

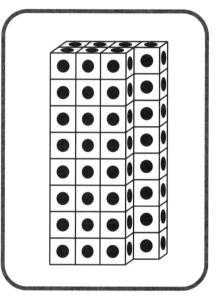

A connecting cube tower

As we review, you can help at home. For example:

- Encourage your child to bring home any math games we played this year. The rules for most of the games are in the *Student Guide,* and many of the materials can be found at home.

- Ask your child to bring home his or her *Multiplication Facts I Know* chart and flash cards. Work with your child to review the multiplication facts. Knowledge of the multiplication facts will be assessed as part of this unit.

- Talk with your child about the experiments we did this year. What were his or her favorites? Why? How were the labs like one another? How were they different?

- Review your child's portfolio together. Ask what he or she learned this year in math.

Thank you for working with me throughout the year.

Sincerely,

_____

Carta al hogar

Fecha : _____

Estimado miembro de familia:

En esta época del año es importante echar una mirada hacia atrás y evaluar el progreso de los estudiantes en matemáticas. Las actividades de esta última unidad permiten repasar y evaluar los conceptos y las habilidades en los que trabajamos todo el año. Dos de las evaluaciones son similares a actividades e investigaciones que los estudiantes hicieron durante el año y dos son exámenes tradicionales. También revisaremos y completaremos nuestros portafolios.

En esta unidad, investigamos la relación entre la altura de una torre hecha con cubos y su volumen. Usando esta información, deberíamos poder decir el volumen de una torre si sabemos la altura o viceversa. Mientras su hijo/a trabaja en la investigación y en las otras actividades, se evaluará su conocimiento del contenido matemático y también su habilidad para resolver problemas y comunicar resultados y soluciones.

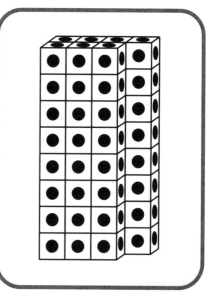

Una torre de cubos conectados

Mientras repasamos, usted puede ayudar en casa. Por ejemplo, puede hacer las siguientes actividades:

- Alentar a su hijo/a a llevar a casa cualquier juego de matemáticas que jugamos este año. Las reglas de la mayoría de los juegos están en la Guía para el estudiante, y muchos de los materiales para los juegos son objetos comunes que encontrará en su casa.

- Pedirle a su hijo/a que lleve a casa "Las tablas que conozco" sobre la multiplicación y las tarjetas para practicar. Ayude a su hijo/a a repasar las tablas de multiplicación. El conocimiento de las tablas de multiplicación se evaluará como parte de esta unidad.

- Hablar con su hijo/a acerca de los experimentos que hicimos este año. ¿Cuáles fueron sus favoritos? ¿Por qué? ¿En qué se parecían los experimentos? ¿En qué se diferenciaban?

- Revisar juntos el portafolio de su hijo/a. Pregúntele a su hijo/a qué aprendió en la clase de matemáticas este año.

Gracias por colaborar conmigo durante todo el año.

Atentamente,

_____

Table of Contents

Unit 20
Connections: An Assessment Unit

Unit 20

Outline

Connections: An Assessment Unit

Unit Summary

This unit provides summative evaluation information by engaging students in several tasks. As in the previous assessment units, Units 2 and 10, students complete both paper-and-pencil and hands-on activities. A class discussion of the labs completed during the year sets the stage for the final lab, *Tower Power*. Use the shorter activity, *Earning Money,* to assess students' abilities to solve an open-response problem and to communicate their problem-solving strategies. Two traditional paper-and-pencil tests and a review of student portfolios are also part of this assessment menu. Students are given many opportunities within this unit to demonstrate the many concepts and skills they have developed over the year. The DPP for this unit assesses all the multiplication facts.

Major Concept Focus

- TIMS Laboratory Method
- variables
- fixed variables
- point graphs
- interpreting graphs
- measuring length in centimeters
- measuring area in square centimeters
- measuring volume in cubic centimeters
- predicting
- money
- division concepts
- communicating problem-solving solutions
- assessing problem solving
- assessing the subtraction facts
- end-of-year test
- DPP assessment of all the multiplication facts

Assessment Indicators

Use the following Assessment Indicators and the *Observational Assessment Record* to assess students on key ideas in the unit.

A1. Are students able to find the area of the base, volume, and height of a cube model?

A2. Can students collect, organize, graph, and analyze data?

A3. Can students make and interpret point graphs?

A4. Can students use patterns in data tables and graphs to make predictions and solve problems?

A5. Can students solve open-response problems and communicate solution strategies?

A6. Can students solve problems involving money?

A7. Do students demonstrate fluency with all the multiplication facts?

Unit Planner

	Lesson Information	Supplies	Copies/ Transparencies
Lesson 1 **Experiment Review** URG Pages 19–27 SG Page 301 DPP A–B HP Part 1 *Estimated Class Sessions* **1**	**Activity** Students review the labs they completed during the year. **Homework** 1. Assign Home Practice Part 1. 2. Assign the multiplication facts as homework for students to review.	• poster board or large sheet of paper for class chart • student portfolios	• 1 transparency of *Stencilrama Graph* URG Page 26 • 1 transparency of a student's point graph from an experiment such as Unit 9 *Mass vs. Number,* optional
Lesson 2 **Tower Power** URG Pages 28–40 DAB Pages 279–287 DPP C–H *Estimated Class Sessions* **3**	**Assessment Lab** Students investigate the relationship between the height and volume of a tower made from centimeter connecting cubes. They graph data and use the graph to make predictions about the heights and volumes of larger towers. **Math Facts** DPP Bit E discusses multiplication facts strategies. **Homework** 1. Assign the Homework section in the *Discovery Assignment Book.* 2. Remind students to study the multiplication facts using the *Triangle Flash Cards.* **Assessment** Review and assess the lab based on the criteria outlined in the Lesson Guide.	• 40 centimeter connecting cubes per student group and 250 additional cubes available for checking predictions • 1 ruler per student • 1 calculator per student	• 1 copy of *Observational Assessment Record* URG Pages 9–10 to be used throughout this unit
Lesson 3 **Becca's Towers** URG Pages 41–48 DPP I–J HP Part 2 *Estimated Class Sessions* **1**	**Assessment Activity** Students solve word problems about cube towers. They graph and interpret information from a data table. **Math Facts** DPP Task J asks students to solve multiplication problems using skip counting. **Homework** Assign Home Practice Part 2. **Assessment** Use the *Observational Assessment Record* to record students' abilities to make and interpret a point graph. Transfer appropriate information from the Unit 20 *Observational Assessment Record* to students' *Individual Assessment Record Sheets.*	• 1 calculator per student • centimeter connecting cubes, optional	• 1 copy of *Becca's Towers* URG Page 45 per student • 1 copy of *Centimeter Graph Paper* URG Page 46 per student • 1 copy of *Individual Assessment Record Sheet* TIG Assessment section per student, previously copied for use throughout the year

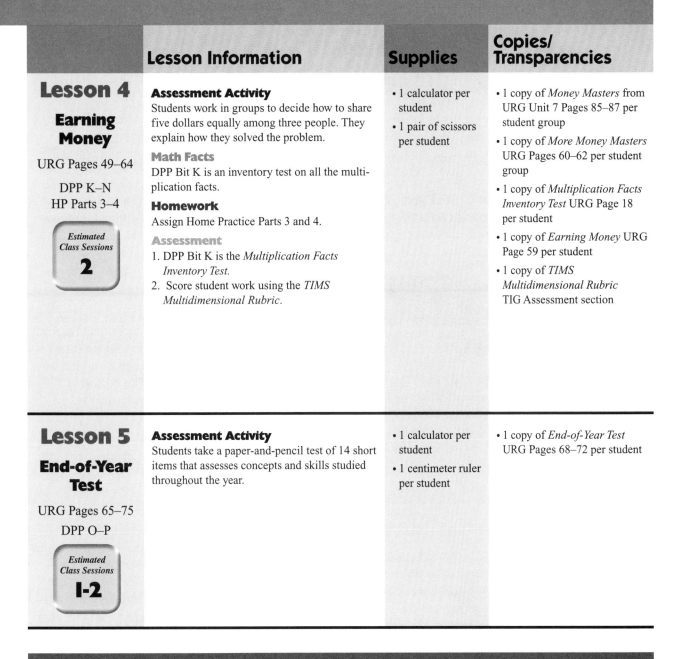

	Lesson Information	Supplies	Copies/Transparencies
Lesson 4 **Earning Money** URG Pages 49–64 DPP K–N HP Parts 3–4 *Estimated Class Sessions* **2**	**Assessment Activity** Students work in groups to decide how to share five dollars equally among three people. They explain how they solved the problem. **Math Facts** DPP Bit K is an inventory test on all the multiplication facts. **Homework** Assign Home Practice Parts 3 and 4. **Assessment** 1. DPP Bit K is the *Multiplication Facts Inventory Test.* 2. Score student work using the *TIMS Multidimensional Rubric.*	• 1 calculator per student • 1 pair of scissors per student	• 1 copy of *Money Masters* from URG Unit 7 Pages 85–87 per student group • 1 copy of *More Money Masters* URG Pages 60–62 per student group • 1 copy of *Multiplication Facts Inventory Test* URG Page 18 per student • 1 copy of *Earning Money* URG Page 59 per student • 1 copy of *TIMS Multidimensional Rubric* TIG Assessment section
Lesson 5 **End-of-Year Test** URG Pages 65–75 DPP O–P *Estimated Class Sessions* **1-2**	**Assessment Activity** Students take a paper-and-pencil test of 14 short items that assesses concepts and skills studied throughout the year.	• 1 calculator per student • 1 centimeter ruler per student	• 1 copy of *End-of-Year Test* URG Pages 68–72 per student

Connections

A current list of literature and software connections is available at *www.mathtrailblazers.com.* You can also find information on connections in the *Teacher Implementation Guide* Literature List and Software List sections.

Software Connections

- *Building Perspective Deluxe* develops spatial reasoning and visual thinking in three dimensions.
- *Graphers* is a data graphing tool appropriate for young students.
- *Kid Pix* allows students to create their own illustrations.
- *MicroWorlds EX* is a drawing program that helps students develop spatial reasoning and an understanding of coordinates while making shapes.
- *Mighty Math Calculating Crew* poses short answer questions about number operations, three-dimensional shapes, and money.

Teaching All Math Trailblazers Students

Math Trailblazers® lessons are designed for students with a wide range of abilities. The lessons are flexible and do not require significant adaptation for diverse learning styles or academic levels. However, when needed, lessons can be tailored to allow students to engage their abilities to the greatest extent possible while building knowledge and skills.

To assist you in meeting the needs of all students in your classroom, this section contains information about some of the features in the curriculum that allow all students access to mathematics. For additional information, see the Teaching the *Math Trailblazers* Student: Meeting Individual Needs section in the *Teacher Implementation Guide*.

Differentiation Opportunities in this Unit

Laboratory Experiments

Laboratory experiments enable students to solve problems using a variety of representations including pictures, tables, graphs, and symbols. Teachers can assign or adapt parts of the analysis according to the student's ability. The following lesson is a lab:

- Lesson 2 *Tower Power*

Journal Prompts

Journal prompts provide opportunities for students to explain and reflect on mathematical problems. They can help both students who need practice explaining their ideas and students who benefit from answering higher order questions. Students with various learning styles can express themselves using pictures, words, and sentences. Teachers can alter journal prompts to suit student's ability levels. The following lessons contain a journal prompt:

- Lesson 1 *Experiment Review*
- Lesson 2 *Tower Power*
- Lesson 4 *Earning Money*

DPP Challenges

DPP Challenges are items from the Daily Practice and Problems that usually take more than fifteen minutes to complete. These problems are more thought-provoking and can be used to stretch students' problem-solving skills. The following lessons have a DPP Challenge in them:

- DPP Challenge B from Lesson 1: *Experiment Review*
- DPP Challenge D from Lesson 2: *Tower Power*

Extensions

Use extensions to enrich lessons. Many extensions provide opportunities to further involve or challenge students of all abilities. Take a moment to review the extensions prior to beginning this unit. Some extensions may require additional preparation and planning. The following lesson contains an extension:

- Lesson 3 *Becca's Towers*

Background
Connections: An Assessment Unit

This unit parallels the midyear assessment in Unit 10 *Numbers and Patterns: An Assessment Unit.* Both of these units provide a variety of assessment tasks that document your students' progress throughout the year. Since each activity in this unit is similar to an activity in Unit 10, students' work can be compared to their work on similar tasks at midyear. The results of these assessments, combined with information you have gathered through daily observations, will result in a comprehensive and balanced picture of their learning.

The unit begins with a review of the labs students completed during the year. This review gives students an opportunity to reflect on the math and science concepts common to all the experiments. The class discussion in this first lesson will set the stage for the final lab in Lesson 2 *Tower Power.* As students work on this experiment, you can assess their abilities to work on a task that extends over several days and requires the application of many

concepts and procedures. Use the shorter activity, *Earning Money,* to assess students' abilities to apply their knowledge of the operations in a problem-solving situation and then to communicate their problem-solving strategies.

Two traditional tests are also part of this assessment menu. Since fluency with the multiplication facts is a goal of the third-grade curriculum, a test of all the multiplication facts is included in this final unit. The other test consists of short items designed to test important procedures, concepts, and skills studied in previous units.

The end of this unit is an appropriate time to review students' portfolios. Students can review and organize their portfolios to assess their own growth and to share their progress with their parents. For more information on portfolios, see the TIMS Tutor: *Portfolios* in the *Teacher Implementation Guide.*

Observational Assessment Record

A1 Are students able to find the area of the base, volume, and height of a cube model?

A2 Can students collect, organize, graph, and analyze data?

A3 Can students make and interpret point graphs?

A4 Can students use patterns in data tables and graphs to make predictions and solve problems?

A5 Can students solve open-response problems and communicate solution strategies?

A6 Can students solve problems involving money?

A7 Do students demonstrate fluency with all the multiplication facts?

A8 _____

Name	A1	A2	A3	A4	A5	A6	A7	A8	Comments
1.									
2.									
3.									
4.									
5.									
6.									
7.									
8.									
9.									
10.									
11.									
12.									
13.									

Name	A1	A2	A3	A4	A5	A6	A7	A8	Comments
14.									
15.									
16.									
17.									
18.									
19.									
20.									
21.									
22.									
23.									
24.									
25.									
26.									
27.									
28.									
29.									
30.									
31.									
32.									

Unit 20

Daily Practice and Problems

Connections: An Assessment Unit

A DPP Menu for Unit 20

Two Daily Practice and Problems (DPP) items are included for each class session listed in the Unit Outline. A scope and sequence chart for the DPP is in the *Teacher Implementation Guide*.

Icons in the Teacher Notes column designate the subject matter of each DPP item. The first item in each class session is always a Bit and the second is either a Task or Challenge. Each item falls into one or more of the categories listed below. A menu of the DPP items for Unit 20 follows.

N Number Sense	⊞ Computation	⏱ Time	⬗ Geometry
A, C, F, J, L, M, O, P	F, I, L, M, O		N
⁵⁄ₓ₇ Math Facts	$ Money	⊓⊔ Measurement	▨ Data
E, J, K		G, H, N	A–D

Practicing and Assessing the Multiplication Facts

By the end of third grade, students are expected to demonstrate fluency with the multiplication facts. In this unit, students are assessed on all the multiplication facts. Students should review the multiplication facts using the *Triangle Flash Cards* in preparation for the *Multiplication Facts Inventory Test* given in DPP item K. Encourage students to focus their review on the facts they have not circled on their *Multiplication Facts I Know* charts. Students can take home their flash cards for these facts or they can make new cards for these facts using the *Triangle Flash Card Masters* which follow the Home Practice in the *Discovery Assignment Book*.

Triangle Flash Cards for all the multiplication facts groups were distributed in Units 11–15 in the *Discovery Assignment Book*. They are also available in the *Grade 3 Facts Resource Guide*.

For information on the distribution and study of the multiplication facts in Grade 3, see the Daily Practice and Problems Guide for Units 3 and 11. For a detailed explanation of our approach to learning and assessing the math facts in Grade 3, see the *Grade 3 Facts Resource Guide* and for information for Grades K–5, see the TIMS Tutor: *Math Facts* in the *Teacher Implementation Guide*.

 **Daily Practice and Problems**

Students may solve the items individually, in groups, or as a class. The items may also be assigned for homework. The DPPs are also available on the Teacher Resource CD.

Student Questions	Teacher Notes

 Averaging Data

Julie collected the following data at home. Find the median for each number of forks she measured.

N Number of Forks	L Length (in cm)			
	Trial 1	Trial 2	Trial 3	Median
1	15.8 cm	15.8 cm	15.8 cm	
2	31.2 cm	31.5 cm	31.2 cm	
4	62.5 cm	62.5 cm	62.8 cm	
8	125.0 cm	125.2 cm	124.8 cm	

TIMS Bit N

The medians, from top to bottom, are 15.8 cm, 31.2 cm, 62.5 cm, and 125.0 cm.

B **Graphing**

Make a point graph on *Centimeter Graph Paper* using the data from TIMS Bit A.
Do the points form a pattern?

TIMS Challenge

Distribute *Centimeter Graph Paper*. Remind students to label the axes. Have students decide on an appropriate scale. Good choices would be to count by ones on the horizontal axis and by tens on the vertical axis. Encourage students to draw a best-fit line.

C Joe Collects Data

Joe Smart filled in this data table. Moe Smart said to Joe, "You made four mistakes in your table." Can you help Joe find them?

C Container	V Volume (in cm)			
	Trial 1	Trial 2	Trial 3	Median
jar	490	520	486	490
cup	240	206	225	206
mug	284	272	290	272
glass	207	198	104	198

TIMS Bit

1. The units for volume should be cubic centimeters.

2. The median volume for the cup should be 225 cc.

3. The median for the mug should be 284 cc.

4. The value for the third trial in the last row is not reasonable. It is almost half the other two values. Joe should collect some more data.

D Graphing, Again

Make a bar graph on *Centimeter Graph Paper* using the corrected data from TIMS Bit C.

TIMS Challenge

Distribute *Centimeter Graph Paper*. Remind students to label their axes.

Have students decide on the scale. A good choice is to go by 25s on the vertical axis.

E Multiplication Facts

1. Which two multiplication facts were the hardest for you to learn?

2. Draw a picture and write a story for these facts. Label your picture with a number sentence.

3. Describe a strategy for each of these facts.

TIMS Bit

Discuss students' strategies. Remind students when you will give the test on all the facts. See DPP Bit K.

Student Questions	Teacher Notes

F Framed Math

Find numbers that will make this sentence true. You can use fractions and decimals.

$$\square + \triangle = 3$$

Make a data table to show your answers.

Your table should have one column for $\square$ and another column for $\triangle$.

TIMS Task

Encourage the use of fractions and decimals. Some possible answers are:

$\square$	$\triangle$
2	1
$2\frac{1}{2}$	$\frac{1}{2}$
$2\frac{2}{3}$	$\frac{1}{3}$

G Mill the Spill

Boo the Blob has a cousin named Mill the Spill. Find Mill's area.

TIMS Bit

Approximately ten sq cm

H Measure to the Nearest Cm

1. Look around you for things of different lengths.

2. Use a cm ruler or tape measure to find their length to the nearest cm.

3. Make a data table showing things you measured and how long each is.

TIMS Task

Students need centimeter rulers to complete this task. You may need to review measuring to the nearest cm.

Student Questions	Teacher Notes

I **Subtraction**

Complete the following problems. Use pencil and paper or mental math to find the answers.

1.　6875　　2.　7015　　3.　896　　4.　2003
　　− 4350　　　　− 2550　　　− 575　　　− 1497

5. Explain a way to do Question 4 in your head.

TIMS Bit ※

1. 2525

2. 4465

3. 321

4. 506

5. Possible strategy: Students can count up from 1497 to 1500 (3), count up from 1500 to 2000 (500), and then 3 more to 2003. $3 + 500 + 3 = 506$.

J **Mathhopper**

If the following mathhoppers start at 0:

1. How many hops would it take for a +7 mathhopper to reach 56?

2. How many hops would it take for a +14 mathhopper to reach 56?

3. How many hops would it take for a +14 mathhopper to reach 560?

TIMS Task N [5×7]

Discuss the variety of strategies students use to solve these problems.

1. 8 hops

2. 4; Since the hop is twice as big as the +7 hop, it will take half as many hops. Skip count by 14 on the calculator or with paper and pencil.

3. 40; In Problem 2 we discovered that $14 \times 4 = 56$. Therefore, $14 \times 40 = 560$.

K **Multiplication Facts Inventory Test**

Have two pens or pencils of different colors ready. Use the first color when you begin the test. Your teacher will tell you when to switch pens or pencils and complete the remaining items with the other color.

TIMS Bit [5×7]

The test can be found at the end of this set of DPP items, following item P. The test includes all the basic multiplication facts. After the test, students should update their *Multiplication Facts I Know* charts. Students should discuss strategies for figuring out or remembering any facts that they do not know well. They can record these strategies in their journals.

Student Questions	Teacher Notes

L Which Two Add Up?

39   276   149   57

1. Which two of these numbers should you add if you want an answer:

   A. over 400?

   B. less than 100?

   C. close to 200?

2. Which number when doubled will be close to 300?

Tell how you decided on your answers. Then, check your answers using base-ten shorthand or pencil and paper.

TIMS Task

1. A. 276 and 149

   B. 57 and 39

   C. 149 and 57 or 149 and 39

2. 149

M Another Mathhopper

A +17 mathhopper starts at 0 and takes 5 hops. Where does it land? Show how you would solve this problem without a calculator.

TIMS Bit

85; students should discuss the strategies they used.

Some may think of 20 × 5 first and work from there. Others may use 17 × 10 and then cut their answer in half. Others may break the 17 into 10 and 7. Some might use addition.

N Dot the Blot

Boo's friend, Dot the Blot, has an area of 10 sq cm.

1. Draw Dot with all straight sides on *Centimeter Graph Paper.*

2. Draw Dot when she does not have straight sides.

TIMS Task

Distribute *Centimeter Graph Paper.* Ask students to fold the paper in half. They can draw one shape on the top half and one on the bottom.

1. Students do not have to draw a rectangle. Accept any shape with straight sides that has an area of 10 sq cm.

2. Remind them of Boo the Blob and that the area they draw will be approximate.

Play Digits: Sums

Draw boxes on your paper like these:

□ □ □
+ □ □
─────

As your teacher or classmate reads the digits, place them in the boxes. Try to find the highest sum. Remember, each digit will be read only once.

TIMS Bit

The directions for Digits can be found in the activity *Digits Game* in Unit 6 Lesson 8 *More Adding and Subtracting*. Discuss the strategies students use to place the digits. How can you make the sum large? If an 8 is read first, where should you put it?

Shaded Shapes

1. Is $\frac{1}{3}$ of the triangle shaded? Explain why or why not.

2. Is $\frac{1}{4}$ of the rectangle shaded? Explain why or why not.

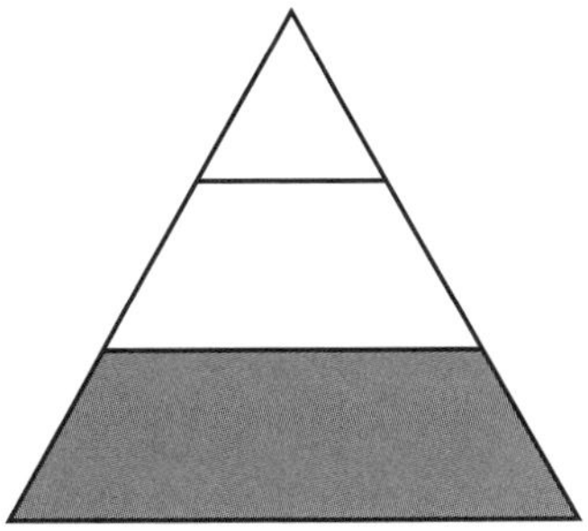

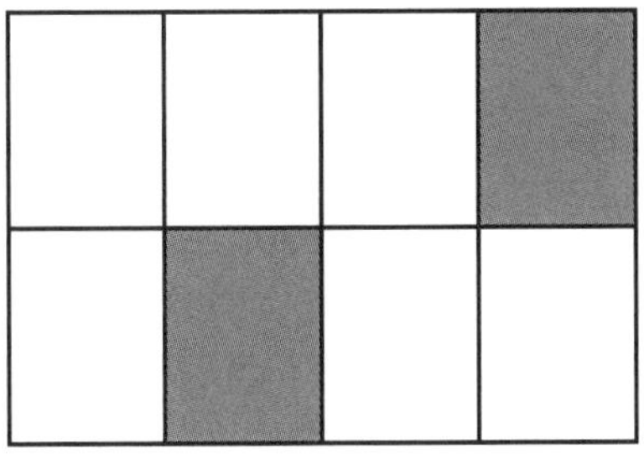

TIMS Task

1. No, the whole triangle is not divided into 3 equal parts.

2. Yes, $\frac{2}{8} = \frac{1}{4}$; if you move the shaded part that is in the corner so that it is above the other shaded part, it is easier to see $\frac{1}{4}$.

Name _____   Date _____

Multiplication Facts
Inventory Test

Directions: You will need two pens or pencils of different colors. Use the first color when you begin the test. When your teacher tells you to switch pens or pencils, finish the test using the second color.

5 ×5	4 ×6	10 ×7	5 ×3	8 ×7
2 ×10	7 ×7	10 ×3	7 ×4	6 ×9
6 ×6	9 ×5	5 ×2	4 ×5	8 ×8
6 ×10	4 ×2	3 ×8	2 ×7	10 ×10
10 ×9	4 ×4	9 ×9	8 ×2	8 ×4
6 ×7	9 ×4	10 ×5	3 ×3	7 ×5
7 ×9	8 ×6	2 ×3	3 ×6	9 ×3
10 ×4	9 ×8	6 ×5	3 ×4	7 ×3
9 ×2	5 ×8	2 ×2	10 ×8	6 ×2

Lesson 1

Experiment Review

Lesson Overview

Students review the labs they worked on during the past year by recounting various elements of each lab: variables, number of trials, type of graph, problems solved, etc. The class discusses the experiments and describes differences and similarities.

Key Content

- Comparing and contrasting the following elements of experiments:

  variables

  measurement procedures

  number of trials

  types of graphs

  problems solved

Key Vocabulary

- bar graph
- point graph
- trial
- variable

Homework

1. Assign Home Practice Part 1.
2. Assign the multiplication facts as homework for students to review.

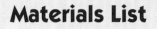
Supplies and Copies

Student	Teacher
Supplies for Each Student • student portfolios	**Supplies** • poster board or large sheet of paper for class chart
Copies	**Copies/Transparencies** • 1 transparency of *Stencilrama Graph* (*Unit Resource Guide* Page 26) • 1 transparency of a student's point graph from an experiment such as Unit 9 *Mass vs. Number,* optional

All blackline masters including assessment, transparency, and DPP masters are also on the Teacher Resource CD.

Student Books

Experiment Review (*Student Guide* Page 301)
Triangle Flash Card Master (*Discovery Assignment Book* Pages 275–277)

Daily Practice and Problems and Home Practice

DPP items A–B (*Unit Resource Guide* Page 12)
Home Practice Part 1 (*Discovery Assignment Book* Page 272)

Note: Classrooms whose pacing differs significantly from the suggested pacing of the units should use the Math Facts Calendar in Section 4 of the *Facts Resource Guide* to ensure students receive the complete math facts program.

Daily Practice and Problems

Suggestions for using the DPPs are on page 24.

A. Bit: Averaging Data (URG p. 12)

Julie collected the following data at home. Find the median for each number of forks she measured.

N Number of Forks	L Length (in cm)			
	Trial 1	Trial 2	Trial 3	Median
1	15.8 cm	15.8 cm	15.8 cm	
2	31.2 cm	31.5 cm	31.2 cm	
4	62.5 cm	62.5 cm	62.8 cm	
8	125.0 cm	125.2 cm	124.8 cm	

B. Challenge: Graphing (URG p. 12)

Make a point graph on *Centimeter Graph Paper* using the data from TIMS Bit A. Do the points form a pattern?

Teaching the Activity

The opening paragraph on the *Experiment Review* Activity Page provides a context for a class discussion reviewing the labs completed during the year. Professor Peabody is reminded of the assessment lab *Stencilrama* from Unit 10 as he uses a stencil to make a border around the top of his living room wall.

As part of the activity, the class will list the labs they completed throughout the year. Then assign each lab to a group of students for review. Start the review with a whole class discussion about *Stencilrama*. Analyze *Stencilrama* as an example by using **Question 2** from the *Experiment Review* Activity Page as a guide. The *Stencilrama Graph* Transparency Master will help you review the lab. **Question 3** then asks students to use the picture on the unit's first page and their portfolios to list the labs they remember working on during the year and to use **Question 2** to structure the analysis of the lab assigned to them.

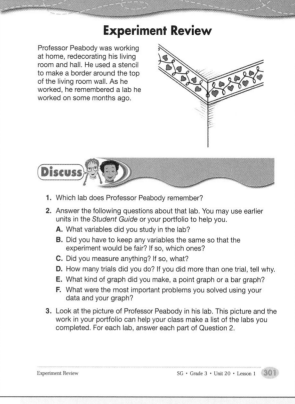

Experiment Review

Professor Peabody was working at home, redecorating his living room and hall. He used a stencil to make a border around the top of the living room wall. As he worked, he remembered a lab he worked on some months ago.

Discuss

1. Which lab does Professor Peabody remember?
2. Answer the following questions about that lab. You may use earlier units in the *Student Guide* or your portfolio to help you.
   A. What variables did you study in the lab?
   B. Did you have to keep any variables the same so that the experiment would be fair? If so, which ones?
   C. Did you measure anything? If so, what?
   D. How many trials did you do? If you did more than one trial, tell why.
   E. What kind of graph did you make, a point graph or a bar graph?
   F. What were the most important problems you solved using your data and your graph?
3. Look at the picture of Professor Peabody in his lab. This picture and the work in your portfolio can help your class make a list of the labs you completed. For each lab, answer each part of Question 2.

Experiment Review   SG • Grade 3 • Unit 20 • Lesson 1   301

Student Guide **- page 301** *(Answers on p. 27)*

After all groups complete their reviews, each should make a report to the class. Organize the information from the reports on a class chart similar to the one in Figure 1. Note that sample responses to **Question 2** for *Stencilrama* are shown in the first column of the chart. A chart similar to this one will provide the data necessary for a class discussion comparing and contrasting labs.

Table of Sample Responses to Student Guide Questions Comparing Selected Experiments

Experiment's Elements	Unit 10 *Stencilrama*	Unit 1 *Kind of Bean*	Unit 5 *The Better "Picker Upper"*	Unit 9 *Mass vs. Number*	Unit 15 *Length vs. Number*	Unit 16 *Fill 'er Up!*
Main Variables	number of stencils, length of border	kind of bean, number of beans	type of paper towel, area of spot	number of objects, mass	number of objects, length of row	containers, volume
Fixed Variables	size and shape of stencils, the orientation of the stencil	size of scoop	number of drops, eye-dropper, position of towels (off desk)	size and shape of objects	size and shape of objects, the way the objects were placed	method of measuring
Anything Measured? (units)	length of border (in)	nothing measured—beans are counted	area of spots (sq cm)	mass of the objects (g)	length of row (cm)	volume (cc)
Number of Trials	1	1	3	1	Answers will vary; 3 is likely.	3
Type of Graph	point	bar	bar	point	point	bar
Problems (Answers will vary.)	predicted length of border for different numbers of stencils	predicted number of each kind of bean in a scoop	predicted number of drops of water to cover the whole towel	predicted mass of different numbers of objects	predicted length of rows of different numbers of objects	predicted number of small containers needed to fill the larger

Figure 1: *A sample experiment review class chart*

After all groups have reported to the class and the information is displayed, continue the discussion with the following questions:

- *When doing an experiment, why do you need to keep some variables fixed?* To be able to look for patterns and make predictions involving the two main variables in an experiment, other variables must be held fixed. For example, to be able to make predictions about the length of a border made with a given number of stencils, the size, shape, and orientation of the stencil must be the same each time it is used. Students often think of holding variables in an experiment fixed as "keeping the experiment fair." In *The Better "Picker Upper,"* students were trying to find the most absorbent paper towel by measuring the area of spots of water. To keep the experiment fair, it was necessary to keep the number of drops the same.

- *Why is it often a good idea to do more than one trial?* One reason scientists use multiple trials is to check on large errors in measurement and in controlling fixed variables. Error is often inevitable, so scientists use multiple trials so they can average out the error. However, if large measurement errors are not likely, one trial may suffice. For example, one measurement was all that was needed to collect accurate data in *Stencilrama* because each time the stencil was used, the border grew exactly 3 inches.

- *How were point graphs used to make predictions?* If the points are close to a straight line, a line can be drawn which fits the points. The line can be used to make predictions. (Show a student's point graph from one of the experiments in which the student drew a line and made a prediction or use the *Stencilrama Graph* transparency as an example.)

- *Name two experiments that are alike. How are they alike? How are they different?* (You can ask this question more than once.) *Stencilrama* and *Mass vs. Number* are alike. In both experiments, students make predictions by measuring a small number of identical objects. Then they predicted a measurement for a larger number of objects using the data plotted on a point graph. In *Mass vs. Number,* students measured mass and in *Stencilrama,* students measured length. Students may also say that *The Better "Picker Upper"* is similar to *Fill 'er Up!* because they made bar graphs in both experiments. However, in *The Better "Picker Upper,"* they measured area and in *Fill 'er Up!,* they measured volume.

Journal Prompt

Which two experiments did you like the best? Why? How are they alike? How are they different?

Discovery Assignment Book - page 272

Name _____ Date _____

Unit 20 Home Practice

PART 1

1.	2.	3.	4.
70 × 9	877 + 549	51 × 8	551 − 435

5. 400 − 237 = _____   6. 719 + 281 = _____   7. 46 × 3 = _____

8. In the morning, Alex spends 25 minutes getting ready for school, an hour delivering papers, and 15 minutes walking to school. If Alex must be at school by 8:00, what time should he wake up?

Show your work. _____

PART 2

1.	2.	3.	4.	5.	6.
893 − 5	893 − 95	893 − 495	645 + 6	645 + 86	645 + 986

7. Explain a strategy for solving Question 2 in your head.

8. A. At the movies, Roberto's mom spent $5.75 on two drinks and one bag of popcorn. If each drink costs $1.75, how much did the popcorn cost?

B. If she paid with a ten-dollar bill, how much change should Roberto's mom get back?

272 DAB · Grade 3 · Unit 20   CONNECTIONS: AN ASSESSMENT UNIT

Math Facts

Inform students when you will give the test on all the multiplication facts. This test is administered in DPP Bit K. Students can practice the facts using *Triangle Flash Cards,* concentrating on those facts they have not circled on their *Multiplication Facts I Know* charts. They can take their *Triangle Flash Cards* home or they can make new ones using the *Triangle Flash Card Masters* that follow the Home Practice in the *Discovery Assignment Book.* Flash cards for the multiplication facts groups are available in the *Grade 3 Facts Resource Guide.*

Homework and Practice

- DPP Bit A asks students to find medians of data in a table and Challenge B asks them to graph the data. Students will need *Centimeter Graph Paper* for Challenge B.

- Home Practice Part 1 provides practice with multiplication, addition, and subtraction computation.

Answers for Part 1 of the Home Practice are in the Answer Key at the end of this lesson and at the end of this unit.

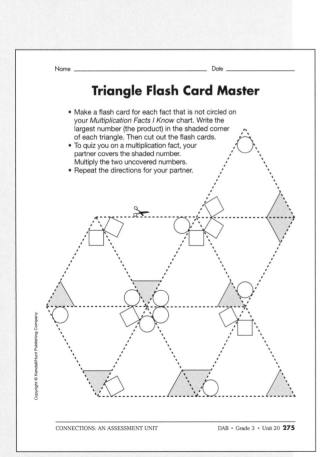

Name _____ Date _____

Triangle Flash Card Master

- Make a flash card for each fact that is not circled on your *Multiplication Facts I Know* chart. Write the largest number (the product) in the shaded corner of each triangle. Then cut out the flash cards.
- To quiz you on a multiplication fact, your partner covers the shaded number. Multiply the two uncovered numbers.
- Repeat the directions for your partner.

CONNECTIONS: AN ASSESSMENT UNIT   DAB · Grade 3 · Unit 20 275

Discovery Assignment Book - page 275

At a Glance

Math Facts and Daily Practice and Problems

DPP Bit A and Challenge B ask students to analyze and graph a set of data.

Teaching the Activity

1. Students review the *Stencilrama* lab with the help of the *Experiment Review* Activity Page in the *Student Guide*.
2. Students review other labs completed throughout the year with the help of the *Experiment Review* Activity Page and their portfolios.
3. Students create a data table showing the components and attributes of completed labs.
4. Students compare and contrast labs to find similarities and differences.

Homework

1. Assign Home Practice Part 1.
2. Assign the multiplication facts as homework for students to review.

Answer Key is on page 27.

Notes:

Stencilrama Graph

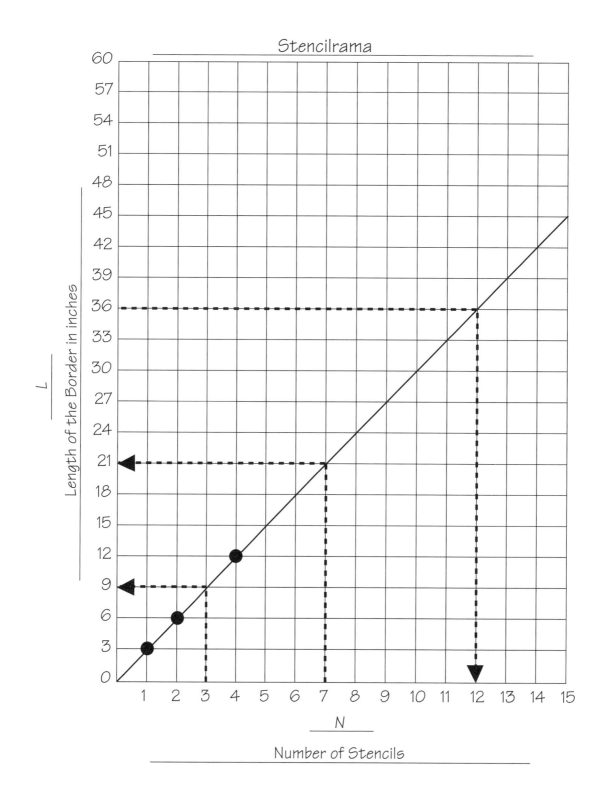

Student Guide (p. 301)

Experiment Review*

I. Stencilrama

2. A. number of stencils; length of border

    B. size and shape of stencils, the orientation of the stencil

    C. length of border in inches

    D. 1 trial

    E. point graph

    F. Answers may vary. We predicted the length of a border for different numbers of stencils.

3. See Figure 1 in the Lesson Guide.

Experiment Review

Professor Peabody was working at home, redecorating his living room and hall. He used a stencil to make a border around the top of the living room wall. As he worked, he remembered a lab he worked on some months ago.

Discuss

1. Which lab does Professor Peabody remember?

2. Answer the following questions about that lab. You may use earlier units in the *Student Guide* or your portfolio to help you.
   A. What variables did you study in the lab?
   B. Did you have to keep any variables the same so that the experiment would be fair? If so, which ones?
   C. Did you measure anything? If so, what?
   D. How many trials did you do? If you did more than one trial, tell why.
   E. What kind of graph did you make, a point graph or a bar graph?
   F. What were the most important problems you solved using your data and your graph?

3. Look at the picture of Professor Peabody in his lab. This picture and the work in your portfolio can help your class make a list of the labs you completed. For each lab, answer each part of Question 2.

Experiment Review   SG • Grade 3 • Unit 20 • Lesson 1   301

Student Guide - page 301

Discovery Assignment Book (p. 272)

Home Practice†

Part 1

I. 630

2. 1426

3. 408

4. 116

5. 163

6. 1000

7. 138

8. 6:20 A.M.

Name _____ Date _____

Unit 20 Home Practice

PART 1

1.	2.	3.	4.
70 × 9	877 + 549	51 × 8	551 − 435

5. $400 - 237 =$ _____   6. $719 + 281 =$ _____   7. $46 \times 3 =$ _____

8. In the morning, Alex spends 25 minutes getting ready for school, an hour delivering papers, and 15 minutes walking to school. If Alex must be at school by 8:00, what time should he wake up?

Show your work. _____

PART 2

1.	2.	3.	4.	5.	6.
893 − 5	893 − 95	893 − 495	645 + 6	645 + 86	645 + 986

7. Explain a strategy for solving Question 2 in your head.

8. A. At the movies, Roberto's mom spent $5.75 on two drinks and one bag of popcorn. If each drink costs $1.75, how much did the popcorn cost?

   B. If she paid with a ten-dollar bill, how much change should Roberto's mom get back?

272 DAB • Grade 3 • Unit 20   CONNECTIONS: AN ASSESSMENT UNIT

Discovery Assignment Book - page 272

*Answers and/or discussion are included in the Lesson Guide.
†Answers for all the Home Practice in the *Discovery Assignment Book* are at the end of the unit.

Lesson 2

Tower Power

Lesson Overview

As students work on this lab, they assume the role of architects for Tiny TIMS Town. They work in groups to design an office tower for the town. While keeping the area of the floor plan fixed, students investigate the relationship between the heights and volumes of towers made from centimeter connecting cubes.

This lab is designed to allow children to make many of their own choices as they work in pairs or small groups. Students design a floor plan for their tower, choose values for the height of several towers, measure the volumes of these towers, organize their data, and graph the data as independently as possible. As the class works on the experiment, you will have an opportunity to assess their abilities to carry out an investigation and to use their data to make predictions and to solve problems.

Key Content

- Finding the area of the base, volume, and height of a cube model.
- Investigating the relationships between height, area, and volume.
- Collecting, organizing, graphing, and analyzing data.
- Using patterns in tables and graphs to make predictions and solve problems.
- Solving problems involving multiplication and division.
- Communicating solution strategies.

Math Facts

DPP Bit E discusses multiplication facts strategies.

Homework

1. Assign the Homework section in the *Discovery Assignment Book.*
2. Remind students to study the multiplication facts using the *Triangle Flash Cards.*

Assessment

Review and assess the lab based on the criteria outlined in the Lesson Guide.

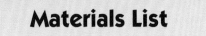

Materials List

Supplies and Copies

Student	Teacher
Supplies for Each Student • ruler • calculator **Supplies for Each Student Group** • 40 centimeter connecting cubes and 250 additional cubes available to the class for checking predictions	**Supplies**
Copies	**Copies/Transparencies** • 1 copy of *Observational Assessment Record* to be used throughout this unit (*Unit Resource Guide* Pages 9–10)

All blackline masters including assessment, transparency, and DPP masters are also on the Teacher Resource CD.

Student Books

Tower Power (*Discovery Assignment Book* Pages 279–287)

Daily Practice and Problems and Home Practice

DPP items C–H (*Unit Resource Guide* Pages 13–14)

Note: Classrooms whose pacing differs significantly from the suggested pacing of the units should use the Math Facts Calendar in Section 4 of the *Facts Resource Guide* to ensure students receive the complete math facts program.

Assessment Tools

Observational Assessment Record (*Unit Resource Guide* Pages 9–10)

C. Bit: Joe Collects Data (URG p. 13)

Joe Smart filled in this data table. Moe Smart said to Joe, "You made four mistakes in your table." Can you help Joe find them?

C Container	V Volume (in cm)			
	Trial 1	Trial 2	Trial 3	Median
jar	490	520	486	490
cup	240	206	225	206
mug	284	272	290	272
glass	207	198	104	198

D. Challenge: Graphing, Again
(URG p. 13)

Make a bar graph on *Centimeter Graph Paper* using the corrected data from TIMS Bit C.

E. Bit: Multiplication Facts (URG p. 13)

1. Which two multiplication facts were the hardest for you to learn?
2. Draw a picture and write a story for these facts. Label your picture with a number sentence.
3. Describe a strategy for each of these facts.

F. Task: Framed Math (URG p. 14)

Find numbers that will make this sentence true. You can use fractions and decimals.

$$\square + \triangle = 3$$

Make a data table to show your answers.

Your table should have one column for $\square$ and another column for $\triangle$.

G. Bit: Mill the Spill (URG p. 14)

Boo the Blob has a cousin named Mill the Spill. Find Mill's area.

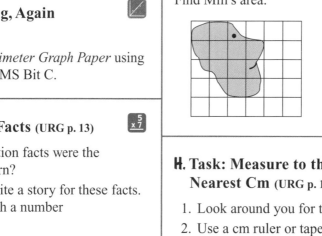

H. Task: Measure to the Nearest Cm (URG p. 14)

1. Look around you for things of different lengths.
2. Use a cm ruler or tape measure to find their length to the nearest cm.
3. Make a data table showing things you measured and how long each is.

Read the lab introduction on the *Tower Power Assessment Pages* in the *Discovery Assignment Book.* This describes the investigation and gives the student architects instructions for designing and building an office tower. The groups begin by choosing a floor plan with an area of 6 square centimeters. Each floor of the office tower will use the same floor plan.

Question 1A asks students about the important variables involved in the lab: Volume, Height, and Area of Floor Plan. *Questions 1B* and *1C* ask which variables change and which stay the same. The height and volume vary from tower to tower. In order to investigate the relationship between height and volume, each group will have to keep the area of the floor plan the same (6 square centimeters) for each tower they build. Following a discussion of *Question 1,* students draw their floor plans on grid paper that is provided on the *Tower Power Assessment Pages.*

After students design a floor plan, they build towers of three different heights, recording the height and volume for each tower in a data table. Student groups should work fairly independently on this lab. Students must choose the three heights for their towers and how to label the two-column data table. Students also can choose how they would like to work. They can either build one tower at a time, recording its data and then taking it apart, or they can build all three towers at once. Since the dimensions of the cubes are precise, one trial should give them accurate data. A blank data table is provided on the *Tower Power* Assessment Pages.

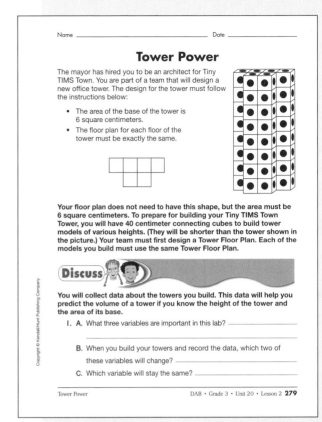

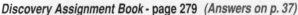

Discovery Assignment Book - page 279 *(Answers on p. 37)*

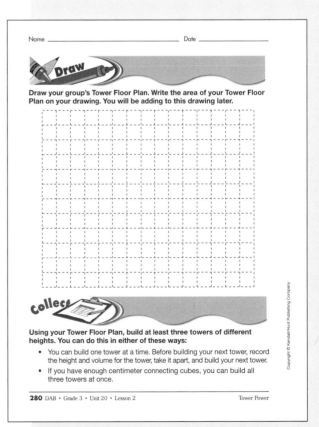

Discovery Assignment Book - page 280 *(Answers on p. 37)*

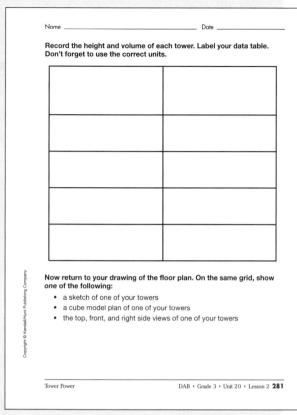

Name _____ Date _____

Record the height and volume of each tower. Label your data table. Don't forget to use the correct units.

Now return to your drawing of the floor plan. On the same grid, show *one* of the following:

- a sketch of one of your towers
- a cube model plan of one of your towers
- the top, front, and right side views of one of your towers

Tower Power   DAB • Grade 3 • Unit 20 • Lesson 2 **281**

Discovery Assignment Book - page 281 *(Answers on p. 37)*

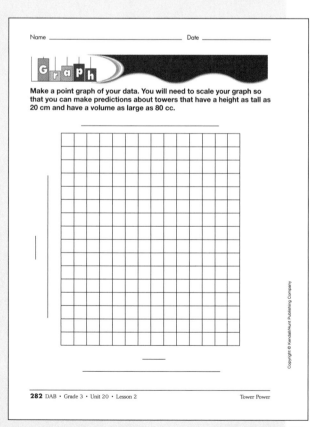

Name _____ Date _____

Make a point graph of your data. You will need to scale your graph so that you can make predictions about towers that have a height as tall as 20 cm and have a volume as large as 80 cc.

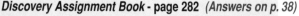

282 DAB • Grade 3 • Unit 20 • Lesson 2   Tower Power

Discovery Assignment Book - page 282 *(Answers on p. 38)*

After the towers are built, students add a two-dimensional representation of one of their towers to their original drawing. They can either draw a sketch, make a cube model plan, or show the top, front, and right side views of one tower. Figure 2 shows a sample drawing of one tower's floor plan, which has an area of 6 square centimeters, and its cube model plan along with the corresponding data table.

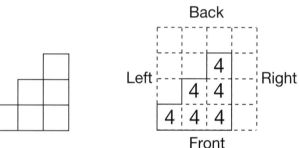

Floor Plan
Area = 6 sq cm

Cube Model Plan

H Height (in cm)	V Volume (in cc)
2 cm	12 cc
4 cm	24 cc
6 cm	36 cc

Figure 2: *Sample data for a tower with a floor plan of 6 square centimeters*

When groups are ready to graph the data, they must decide on appropriate scales for each axis. The *Tower Power* Assessment Pages in the *Discovery Assignment Book* provide guidelines for choosing scales so students will be able to use the graph to make predictions about the volume and height of larger towers. Figure 3 shows a sample graph (including answers for **Questions 3** and **4**). The horizontal axis is scaled by twos and the vertical axis is scaled by fives.

The sample graph in Figure 3 shows how to use the graph to make the predictions that are required for **Questions 3** and **4.** Students are also asked to check their predictions without using their graphs. Some students may use the cubes to build towers; others may use multiplication or division to solve the problem another way. Both methods are good choices.

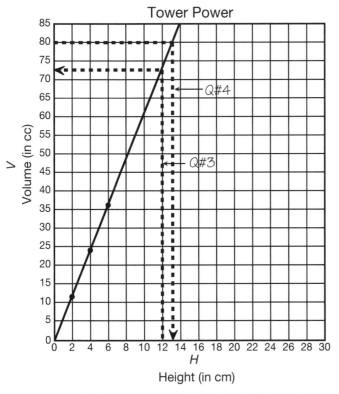

Figure 3: *Sample graph of the data in Figure 2*

A class discussion of the various methods can help students see the relationship between the concrete objects, the graph, and the operations of multiplication and division.

To solve **Question 4B,** students may skip count by sixes (the number of cubes in each floor) on a calculator 13 times to reach 78. There will be two cubes left over. If students use division to solve this problem, they will need to know how to interpret the remainder. Using a calculator $80 \div 6 = 13.333333$. Students should understand that the 3s to the right of the decimal point indicate a remainder, but not enough to make another whole floor.

Questions 5 and **6** ask the students to make predictions about very large towers without using their cubes or graphs to find the values. These questions provide an opportunity for students to solve problems using multiplication and division.

Journal Prompt

Which labs are like Tower Power? How are they alike? How are they different?

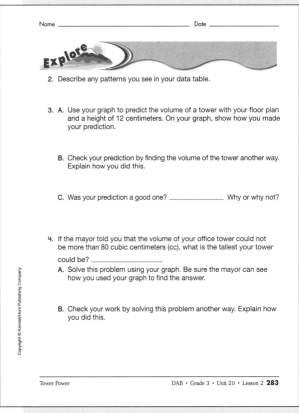

Name _____ Date _____

Explore

2. Describe any patterns you see in your data table.

3. A. Use your graph to predict the volume of a tower with your floor plan and a height of 12 centimeters. On your graph, show how you made your prediction.

   B. Check your prediction by finding the volume of the tower another way. Explain how you did this.

   C. Was your prediction a good one? _____ Why or why not?

4. If the mayor told you that the volume of your office tower could not be more than 80 cubic centimeters (cc), what is the tallest your tower could be? _____
   A. Solve this problem using your graph. Be sure the mayor can see how you used your graph to find the answer.

   B. Check your work by solving this problem another way. Explain how you did this.

Tower Power   DAB • Grade 3 • Unit 20 • Lesson 2 **283**

Discovery Assignment Book - page 283 (Answers on p. 38)

Name _____ Date _____

5. The tallest office building in the United States is the Sears Tower in Chicago. It has 110 floors. If a tower with your floor plan had 110 floors, how many cubes would you need to build the tower? _____

   Show how you solved the problem. Write a number sentence for this problem.

   _____

6. The final instructions tell your team that the volume of the office tower should be as close to 600 cc as possible. How tall will your office tower be? _____ Show your work.

284 DAB • Grade 3 • Unit 20 • Lesson 2   Tower Power

Discovery Assignment Book - page 284 (Answers on p. 39)

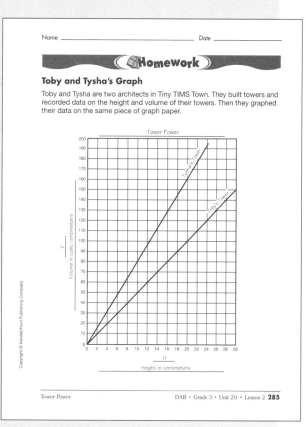

Discovery Assignment Book - page 285

DPP Bit E discusses strategies for multiplication facts that students find difficult.

Homework and Practice

- DPP items C and D ask students to graph and analyze data. Task F asks students to complete a number sentence using fractions. Bit G asks students to estimate area by counting square centimeters and Task H provides practice with measuring to the nearest centimeter.

- Assign the Homework section in the *Discovery Assignment Book.* Students may solve the problems using interpolation, extrapolation, multiplication, or division. To answer *Question 8,* students compare the volume of Toby's and Tysha's towers for any given height. For example, if Toby's tower has a height of ten centimeters, its volume is 50 cc *(Question 1).* Tysha's ten-story tower has a volume of 80 cc *(Question 4).* The floor plan for Tysha's tower must have a larger area.

- To prepare for the *Multiplication Facts Inventory Test* in DPP Bit K, students should review the multiplication facts using flash cards.

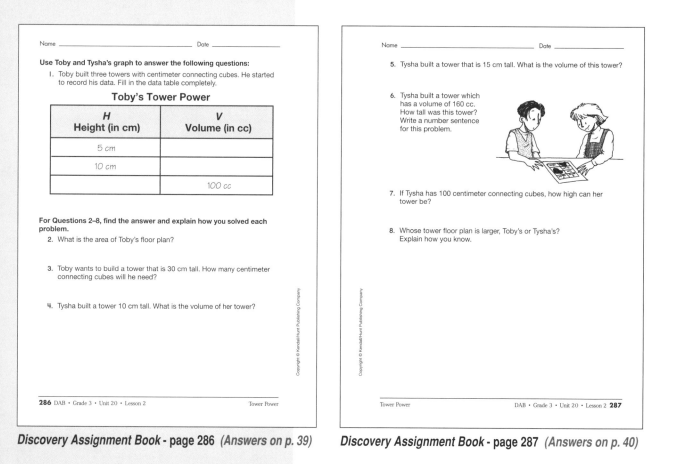

Discovery Assignment Book - page 286 *(Answers on p. 39)*

Discovery Assignment Book - page 287 *(Answers on p. 40)*

Assessment

The lab provides opportunities to observe students' abilities to conduct the various parts of the laboratory investigation and work with data. Record your observations using the *Observational Assessment Record*. You can use the following criteria to assess student abilities in each phase of the lab:

- Drawing a picture
    1. Is the floor plan clearly illustrated?
    2. Have students accurately made a two-dimensional representation of their tower?
- Collecting and recording data
    1. Is the data table well organized and clearly labeled?
    2. Are the correct units of measurement included?
    3. Are the measurements correct?
- Graphing data
    1. Is there a title?
    2. Are the axes scaled correctly and labeled clearly?
    3. Are the data points plotted accurately?
    4. Is the best-fit line drawn properly?
- Solving problems
    1. Are the strategies and solutions clearly communicated?
    2. Are the answers correct based on the data?

Math Facts and Daily Practice and Problems

DPP items C and D ask students to graph and analyze data. Bit E discusses multiplication facts strategies. Task F asks students to complete number sentences. Bit G asks students to estimate area and Task H provides practice with measuring length.

Teaching the Lab

1. Read the lab introduction on the *Tower Power* Assessment Pages in the *Discovery Assignment Book*.
2. Students discuss the important variables of the investigation in **Question 1** on the *Tower Power* Assessment Pages.
3. Groups choose a floor plan with an area of 6 square centimeters.
4. Students draw their floor plans on grid paper.
5. Students use their floor plans to build towers of three different heights, label their data tables, and record the heights and volumes for each tower.
6. Students add a two-dimensional representation of one of their towers to their drawings.
7. Groups decide on appropriate scales for each axis and graph their data.
8. Students complete **Questions 2–6** on the *Tower Power* Assessment Pages.
9. Students use their graphs to make predictions for **Questions 3** and **4** and then check their predictions without using their graphs. Discuss the various methods they use.
10. In **Questions 5** and **6,** students make predictions about very large towers without using their cubes or graphs to find the values. Students may solve these problems using multiplication and division.

Homework

1. Assign the Homework section in the *Discovery Assignment Book*.
2. Remind students to study the multiplication facts using the *Triangle Flash Cards*.

Assessment

Review and assess the lab based on the criteria outlined in the Lesson Guide.

Answer Key is on pages 37–40.

Notes:

Discovery Assignment Book (pp. 279–281)

Tower Power*

See Figures 2 and 3 in the Lesson Guide for a sample picture, data table, and graph.

I. **A.** volume, height, and area of the floor

   B. height and volume

   C. area of floor

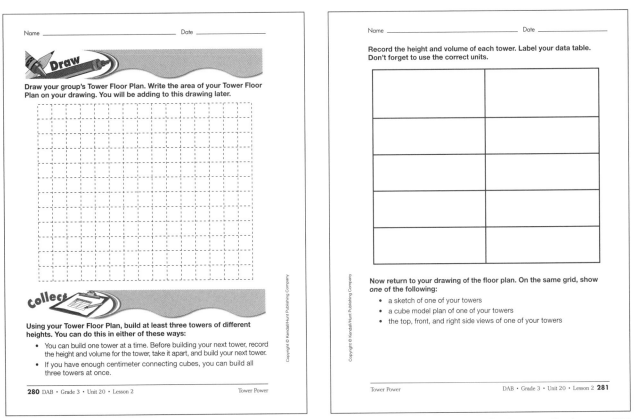

Discovery Assignment Book - page 279

Discovery Assignment Book - page 280

Discovery Assignment Book - page 281

*Answers and/or discussion are included in the Lesson Guide.

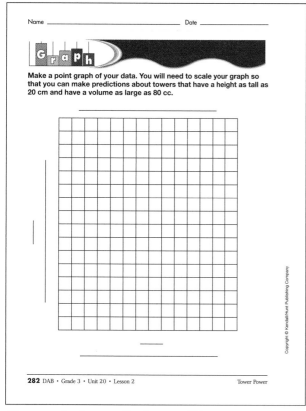

Discovery Assignment Book - page 282

Discovery Assignment Book (pp. 282–283)

2. Answers will vary. The volume of each cube model is a multiple of 6. The volume is 6 times the height.

3. A. 72 cc; the extrapolation is shown on the graph in Figure 3 in the Lesson Guide.

   B. Strategies will vary. $6 \times 12 = 72$ cc; use more cubes if available and actually build the tower with height of 12 centimeters.

   C. Answers will vary. Yes, using the graph I predicted 72 cc which matches my answer in 3B. Also, I checked it by actually building the tower.

4. A. 13 centimeters tall; the volume would be 78 cc; the extrapolation is shown on the graph in Figure 3 in the Lesson Guide.

   B. 13 centimeters tall; $80 \div 6 = 13$ cm and 2 cubes left over; using the calculator students may skip count by sixes (the number of cubes in each floor) 13 times to reach 78. Two cubes will be left over.*

Discovery Assignment Book - page 283

*Answers and/or discussion are included in the Lesson Guide.

Discovery Assignment Book (p. 284)

5. 660 cubes; solution strategies will vary.
$6 \times 110 = 660$ cubes

6. 100 centimeters tall; strategies will vary.
$600 \div 6 = 100$ cm

Name _____ Date _____

5. The tallest office building in the United States is the Sears Tower in Chicago. It has 110 floors. If a tower with your floor plan had 110 floors, how many cubes would you need to build the tower? _____

Show how you solved the problem. Write a number sentence for this problem.

_____

6. The final instructions tell your team that the volume of the office tower should be as close to 600 cc as possible. How tall will your office tower be? _____ Show your work.

284 DAB • Grade 3 • Unit 20 • Lesson 2   Tower Power

Discovery Assignment Book - page 284

Discovery Assignment Book (p. 286)

1.

H Height (in cm)	V Volume (in cc)
5 cm	25 cc
10 cm	50 cc
20 cm	100 cc

2. 5 square centimeters; strategies will vary. Divide any of the volumes by their corresponding heights from the data table or use the graph.

3. 150 cubes; use Toby and Tysha's graph and extrapolate from Toby's line. The volume is 150 cc.

4. 80 cc; use Tysha's line on the graph. The volume is 80 cc.

Name _____ Date _____

Use Toby and Tysha's graph to answer the following questions:

1. Toby built three towers with centimeter connecting cubes. He started to record his data. Fill in the data table completely.

Toby's Tower Power

H Height (in cm)	V Volume (in cc)
5 cm	
10 cm	
	100 cc

For Questions 2–8, find the answer and explain how you solved each problem.

2. What is the area of Toby's floor plan?

3. Toby wants to build a tower that is 30 cm tall. How many centimeter connecting cubes will he need?

4. Tysha built a tower 10 cm tall. What is the volume of her tower?

286 DAB • Grade 3 • Unit 20 • Lesson 2   Tower Power

Discovery Assignment Book - page 286

Name _____ Date _____

5. Tysha built a tower that is 15 cm tall. What is the volume of this tower?

6. Tysha built a tower which has a volume of 160 cc. How tall was this tower? Write a number sentence for this problem.

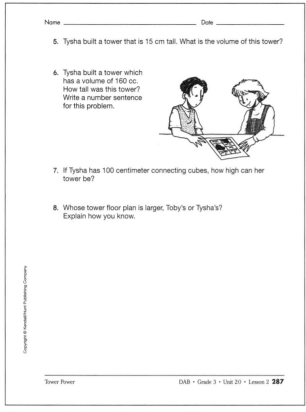

7. If Tysha has 100 centimeter connecting cubes, how high can her tower be?

8. Whose tower floor plan is larger, Toby's or Tysha's? Explain how you know.

Tower Power   DAB • Grade 3 • Unit 20 • Lesson 2 **287**

Discovery Assignment Book - page 287

Discovery Assignment Book (p. 287)

5. 120 cc; use the graph. The volume is 120. Divide the volume of any tower by its corresponding height and you will find that the area of each floor is 8 square centimeters. Then multiply the area of one floor by 15: $8 \times 15 = 120$ cc

6. 20 centimeters; use the graph or division. $(160 \div 8 = 20)$

7. 12 centimeters; use the graph or division. $(100 \div 8 = 12$ and 4 left over; 12 floors of 8 cc each and 4 cubes left over)

8. The area of Tysha's floor plan is larger by 3 square centimeters.*

*Answers and/or discussion are included in the Lesson Guide.

Lesson 3

Becca's Towers

Students use Becca's tower data to make a line graph and solve problems using that data.

Key Content

- Making and interpreting point graphs.
- Using patterns in data tables and graphs to solve problems.
- Communicating solutions verbally and in writing.

Math Facts

DPP Task J asks students to solve multiplication problems using skip counting.

Homework

Assign Home Practice Part 2.

Assessment

Use the *Observational Assessment Record* to record students' abilities to make and interpret a point graph. Transfer appropriate information from the Unit 20 *Observational Assessment Record* to students' *Individual Assessment Record Sheet.*

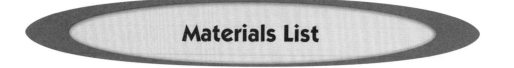

Materials List

Supplies and Copies

Student	Teacher
Supplies for Each Student • calculator • centimeter connecting cubes, optional	**Supplies**
Copies • 1 copy of *Becca's Towers* per student (*Unit Resource Guide* Page 45) • 1 copy of *Centimeter Graph Paper* per student (*Unit Resource Guide* Page 46)	**Copies/Transparencies**

All blackline masters including assessment, transparency, and DPP masters are also on the Teacher Resource CD.

Daily Practice and Problems and Home Practice

DPP items I–J (*Unit Resource Guide* Page 15)
Home Practice Part 2 (*Discovery Assignment Book* Page 272)

Note: Classrooms whose pacing differs significantly from the suggested pacing of the units should use the Math Facts Calendar in Section 4 of the *Facts Resource Guide* to ensure students receive the complete math facts program.

Assessment Tools

Observational Assessment Record (*Unit Resource Guide* Pages 9–10)
Individual Assessment Record Sheet (*Teacher Implementation Guide,* Assessment section)

Daily Practice and Problems

Suggestions for using the DPPs are on page 43.

I. Bit: Subtraction (URG p. 15)

Complete the following problems. Use pencil and paper or mental math to find the answers.

1. $6875 - 4350$ 2. $7015 - 2550$ 3. $896 - 575$ 4. $2003 - 1497$

5. Explain a way to do Question 4 in your head.

J. Task: Mathhopper (URG p. 15)

If the following mathhoppers start at 0:

1. How many hops would it take for a +7 mathhopper to reach 56?
2. How many hops would it take for a +14 mathhopper to reach 56?
3. How many hops would it take for a +14 mathhopper to reach 560?

Teaching the Activity

If *Becca's Towers* is to be used as assessment, students should complete the activity individually in class. Otherwise, students can work on these problems in pairs or in groups. Encourage students to explain how they solved the problems in *Questions 2–5.*

Math Facts

DPP Task J provides practice with jumps on a number line and division.

Homework and Practice

- DPP Bit I provides subtraction practice.
- Home Practice Part 2 provides practice with addition and subtraction.

Answers for Part 2 of the Home Practice are in the Answer Key at the end of this lesson and at the end of this unit.

Assessment

Use the *Observational Assessment Record* to record students' abilities to make and interpret point graphs.

Extension

Ask students to write their own problems using Becca's data. Students should include some problems that use interpolation and others that use extrapolation. Have students exchange problems and share solutions.

Name _____ Date _____

Unit 20 Home Practice

PART 1

1.	2.	3.	4.
70	877	51	551
× 9	+ 549	× 8	− 435

5. 400 − 237 = _____ 6. 719 + 281 = _____ 7. 46 × 3 = _____

8. In the morning, Alex spends 25 minutes getting ready for school, an hour delivering papers, and 15 minutes walking to school. If Alex must be at school by 8:00, what time should he wake up?

Show your work. _____

_____

PART 2

1.	2.	3.	4.	5.	6.
893	893	893	645	645	645
− 5	− 95	− 495	+ 6	+ 86	+ 986

7. Explain a strategy for solving Question 2 in your head.

8. A. At the movies, Roberto's mom spent $5.75 on two drinks and one bag of popcorn. If each drink costs $1.75, how much did the popcorn cost?

   B. If she paid with a ten-dollar bill, how much change should Roberto's mom get back?

272 DAB • Grade 3 • Unit 20   CONNECTIONS: AN ASSESSMENT UNIT

Discovery Assignment Book - page 272 (Answers on p. 47)

At a Glance

Math Facts and Daily Practice and Problems

DPP Bit I provides subtraction practice. Task J asks students to solve multiplication problems using skip counting.

Teaching the Activity

Students complete the *Becca's Towers* Assessment Blackline Master.

Homework

Assign Home Practice Part 2.

Assessment

Use the *Observational Assessment Record* to record students' abilities to make and interpret a point graph. Transfer appropriate information from the Unit 20 *Observational Assessment Record* to students' *Individual Assessment Record Sheets*.

Extension

Ask students to write their own problems using Becca's data.

Answer Key is on pages 47–48.

Notes:

Becca's Towers

Becca built towers out of centimeter connecting cubes. Then she measured the height and volume of each tower. Each tower had the same floor plan for each floor. Here is her data table.

Becca's Towers

H Height (in cm)	V Volume (in cc)
2 cm	6 cc
4 cm	12 cc
8 cm	24 cc

1. Make a point graph of the data on a separate sheet of graph paper. You will need to scale your graph so you can make predictions about towers that are as tall as 30 cm and have a volume as large as 40 cc.

For Questions 2–5, be sure to explain how you solved each problem.

2. **A.** Use your graph to find the volume of a tower that is 12 cm tall and uses Becca's floor plan. On the graph, show how you solved the problem.

   B. Check your work by solving the problem another way. Use a number sentence in your explanation.

3. **A.** Becca is going to make a tower from 28 centimeter connecting cubes. Use your graph to find the height of the tallest tower that Becca can build using her floor plan. On the graph, show how you solved the problem.

   B. Check your work by solving the problem another way. Use a number sentence in your explanation.

4. Becca wants to build a tower that is 50 cm tall. How many centimeter connecting cubes will she need?

5. If Becca has 100 centimeter connecting cubes, how tall can she build a tower using her floor plan?

Centimeter Graph Paper, Blackline Master

Discovery Assignment Book (p. 272)

Home Practice*

Part 2

1. 888

2. 798

3. 398

4. 651

5. 731

6. 1631

7. Possible strategy: $893 - 100 = 793$
$793 + 5 = 798$

8. A. $2.25
   B. $4.25

Name _____ Date _____

Unit 20 Home Practice

PART 1

1.	2.	3.	4.
70 $\times$ 9	877 $+ 549$	51 $\times$ 8	551 $- 435$

5. $400 - 237 =$ _____ 6. $719 + 281 =$ _____ 7. $46 \times 3 =$ _____

8. In the morning, Alex spends 25 minutes getting ready for school, an hour delivering papers, and 15 minutes walking to school. If Alex must be at school by 8:00, what time should he wake up?

Show your work. _____

_____

PART 2

1.	2.	3.	4.	5.	6.
893 $- 5$	893 $- 95$	893 $- 495$	645 $+ 6$	645 $+ 86$	645 $+ 986$

7. Explain a strategy for solving Question 2 in your head.

8. A. At the movies, Roberto's mom spent $5.75 on two drinks and one bag of popcorn. If each drink costs $1.75, how much did the popcorn cost?

B. If she paid with a ten-dollar bill, how much change should Roberto's mom get back?

272 DAB • Grade 3 • Unit 20   CONNECTIONS: AN ASSESSMENT UNIT

Discovery Assignment Book - page 272

---

*Answers for all the Home Practice in the *Discovery Assignment Book* are at the end of the unit.

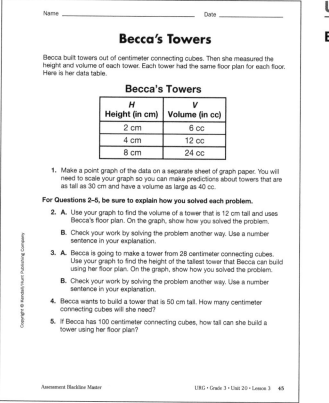

Unit Resource Guide - page 45

Unit Resource Guide (p. 45)

Becca's Towers

1.

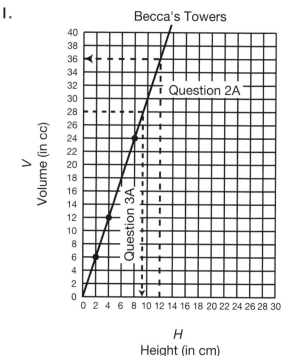

2. **A.** 36 cc

   B. Solution strategies will vary. Divide any of the volumes by their corresponding height and you will find that the area of each floor is 3 sq cm. Then multiply the area of one floor by 12: $3 \times 12 = 36$ cc

3. **A.** 9 centimeters

   B. $28 \div 3 = 9$ cm and 1 cube left over; students may skip count by 3 (number of cubes in each floor) to reach 27. There will be 1 cube left over.

4. 150 cc; $50 \times 3 = 150$ cc

5. 33 centimeters tall; $100 \div 3 = 33$ R1; using a calculator, students may skip count by 3 (number of cubes in each floor) to reach 99. There will be 1 cube left over. If students divide 100 by 3 on the calculator, they will need to know how to interpret the remainder. Using a calculator shows $100 \div 3 = 33.333333$. Students should understand that the 3s to the right of the decimal point indicate a remainder, but will not make another whole floor.

Lesson 4

Earning Money

Lesson Overview

Students must decide how to divide five dollars equally among three people. Play money is made available to students to help them solve the problem. They are also asked to solve the problem using calculators. Students write explanations of how they solved the problem including a description of any tools used.

Key Content

- Solving open-response problems.
- Communicating problem-solving strategies.
- Solving problems involving multiplication and division.
- Interpreting remainders.
- Solving problems involving money.

Math Facts

DPP Bit K is an inventory test on all the multiplication facts.

Homework

Assign Home Practice Parts 3 and 4.

Assessment

1. DPP Bit K is the *Multiplication Facts Inventory Test.*
2. Score student work using the *TIMS Multidimensional Rubric.*

Materials List

Supplies and Copies

Student	Teacher
Supplies for Each Student • calculator • scissors	**Supplies**
Copies • 1 copy of *Multiplication Facts Inventory Test* per student (*Unit Resource Guide* Page 18) • 1 copy of *Earning Money* per student (*Unit Resource Guide* Page 59) • 1 copy of *Money Masters* per student group (*Unit Resource Guide* Unit 7 Pages 85–87) • 1 copy of *More Money Masters* per student group (*Unit Resource Guide* Pages 60–62)	**Copies/Transparencies** • 1 copy of *TIMS Multidimensional Rubric* (*Teacher Implementation Guide,* Assessment Section)

All blackline masters including assessment, transparency, and DPP masters are also on the Teacher Resource CD.

Student Books

Student Rubrics: *Knowing, Solving,* and *Telling* (*Student Guide* Appendices A–C and Inside Back Cover)

Daily Practice and Problems and Home Practice

DPP items K–N (*Unit Resource Guide* Pages 15–16)
Home Practice Parts 3–4 (*Discovery Assignment Book* Page 273)

Note: Classrooms whose pacing differs significantly from the suggested pacing of the units should use the Math Facts Calendar in Section 4 of the *Facts Resource Guide* to ensure students receive the complete math facts program.

Assessment Tools

TIMS Multidimensional Rubric (*Teacher Implementation Guide,* Assessment section)
Observational Assessment Record (*Unit Resource Guide* Pages 9–10)
Individual Assessment Record Sheet (*Teacher Implementation Guide,* Assessment section)

Daily Practice and Problems

Suggestions for using the DPPs are on page 57.

K. Bit: Multiplication Facts Inventory Test (URG p. 15)

$\boxed{\frac{5}{\times 7}}$

Have two pens or pencils of different colors ready. Use the first color when you begin the test. Your teacher will tell you when to switch pens or pencils and complete the remaining items with the other color.

M. Bit: Another Mathhopper (URG p. 16)

A +17 mathhopper starts at 0 and takes 5 hops. Where does it land? Show how you would solve this problem without a calculator.

L. Task: Which Two Add Up? (URG p. 16)

39   276   149   57

1. Which two of these numbers should you add if you want an answer:
   A. over 400?
   B. less than 100?
   C. close to 200?

2. Which number when doubled will be close to 300?

Tell how you decided on your answers. Then, check your answers using base-ten shorthand or pencil and paper.

N. Task: Dot the Blot (URG p. 16)

Boo's friend, Dot the Blot, has an area of 10 sq cm.

1. Draw Dot with all straight sides on *Centimeter Graph Paper*.
2. Draw Dot when she does not have straight sides.

Teaching the Activity

Before students begin working in their groups, the class should read the problem on the *Earning Money* Assessment Blackline Master. Students should understand they have the option of using play money to help them divide the five dollars. Ask them how they can use a calculator to solve the problem. The problem assesses students' abilities to solve an open-response problem involving division and to interpret any remainder.

Note that in the three samples of student work shown, each solution is quite different. All the students had to interpret the remainder in some way, even though they did not necessarily use the division operation to find the answer. One group of students, whose work is not included, correctly solved the problem without having any money left over. They decided to buy bubble gum with the extra 2¢ and to divide the bubble gum into three pieces. Another group of students gave each student $1.50 and then said they would give the remaining 50¢ to the poor. Tell students they must find the smallest possible remainder.

Since the money must be shared among three children, groups of three students work well for this activity. Once groups solve the problem, encourage students to write clear explanations of all strategies used. Each group can write an explanation, or each student can write his or her own report.

To communicate your expectations, review with the class one or more of the student rubrics. Remind them to include a description of how they used calculators, play money, or other tools. If possible, give students an opportunity to revise their work based on your comments. For example, if a student only wrote about using play money, ask him or her to explain what happened when he or she tried a calculator. You may ask another student to include number sentences with his or her explanation.

In the following discussion, you will find three examples of student work with scores for each dimension of the *TIMS Multidimensional Rubric*. To assist you in scoring students' work, questions specific to this task were developed. These questions are grouped within each dimension:

Solving

- Did students' strategies include using a calculator?
- Were students' strategies for dividing the money systematic and efficient?
- Did students organize their work?
- Did they look back at the problem and draw appropriate conclusions about their answers and the remainder?

Knowing

- Did students choose appropriate operations? Students' solutions may involve the following operations:
    1. *Multiplication, repeated subtraction,* or *repeated addition* as part of a guess-and-check strategy
    2. *Division* to divide the money into equal shares
    3. *Subtraction* to find the amount of money left over after each person has received a share
- Did students compute accurately?
- Did students use calculators effectively? If students used calculators to divide, were they able to interpret the decimal portion?
- Were students able to reconcile the solution they found using manipulatives with the solution they found using calculators?

Telling

- Did students clearly describe all their strategies?
- Did students organize their work in a logical way?
- Did they use appropriate number sentences or other symbolic representations?
- Did they discuss any connections between decimals on a calculator, play money, and any real world situations?

Kim's Work

Didn't Work			
Daniel	Maria	Cora	
$1.70	$1.70	$1.70	0 10
$1.60	$1.60	$1.60	R 0
Worked			
Daniel	Maria	Cora	
$1.65	$1.65	$1.65	5R
$1.66	$1.66	$1.66	2R

Kim's response the first day:

$1.66 R2 / $1.66 and 2¢ remaining to give to charity or something like that.
I found my remainder by fidgeting around in my head, finding the answer and
figuring out there's some remaining and I added $1.66 3 times and 2 remained.

$1.66 × 3 = $4.98
It gave us $4.98 and we knew $4.98 + 2 = $5.00 so, there was
2 remaining.

Teacher comments:

Since 1.70 × 3 = 5.10, you would have 10¢ too little—not enough to share
equally. I don't understand the way you wrote your remainders in your
table. Since 1.60 × 3 = 4.80, the remainder would be 20¢, not 0.

Mr. Fish

Kim did not correct her table.

Figure 4: *Kim's work*

Solving, 3

Kim used a guess-and-check strategy and organized
her work in a table. She checked her guesses using a
calculator and looked back at her final answer to make
sure it was reasonable. Although her strategy was
effective, it was not as efficient as it could have been.

Knowing, 3

Kim chose to use multiplication, addition, and subtraction. Most of her calculations are correct, but she
did not always report the remainder correctly when
she displayed her work in her data table. She also did
not correct her table when her teacher pointed this

out. Even though she did not use division, she did
indicate that there would be "2¢ remaining to give to
charity or something like that."

Telling, 3

Kim reported on the use of addition, subtraction, and
multiplication through the use of words, number sentences, and a data table. Each of her number sentences is clear and correct, and the data table is
labeled so that we know which solutions she thinks
"worked" and "didn't work." We are not entirely sure
of her thinking, however, since she tells us she found
her answer by "fidgeting around in my head . . . ."

Marco's Work

Marco's response the first day:

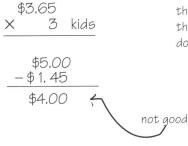

$3.65
×   3   kids

three dollars and sixey five cenes times
three kids, and five dollers minus one
doller and foty five cenes egels fore dollers.

$5.00
− $1.45
$4.00 ← not good

Teacher comments:

I'm still not clear from your explanation what you tried. Maybe you should try to explain to me. Did you use the money or the calculator? Try to finish today.

Ms. Ho

Marco's response the second day:

I didn't use the money, But
I used a calculator.

```
 75¢                    165          $1.70
 75        $4.50        × 3          ×   3
 75        3   ×        4.95         $5.10
───        $1.50
225                     1.67
                        ×  3
  3        3.13         5.01         1.69
$1.10      × 3                       ×  3
$1.10      3.39                      5.07
$1.10                   1.66
+ $3.30                 ×   3
                        4.98
```

Figure 5: *Marco's work*

Solving, 2
Marco also used a guess-and-check strategy, but he made almost no attempt to organize his work in any way. Although his strategy was inefficient, he persisted until he found a solution.

Knowing, 2
Marco chose to use repeated addition and multiplication to check each guess. He never explicitly used subtraction to calculate the amount of money that would be left over, never identifying the remainder. This indicates that he did not completely understand all the mathematical concepts inherent in the problem.

Telling, 1
Marco wrote very little to explain his strategy or thinking. He showed all his trials, but made no attempt to organize them. Since he did not identify which trial was successful, we are not even sure of his final answer.

Jayne's Work

Jayne's response the first day:

1.) Each person should get $1.66 and .2 left over. We got five dollars in change and we divided the money up between them. We got $1.66 for each person, and two cents left over.

2.) If you try on the calculator (5 ÷ 3) you would get 1.6666667. So I think it's much better to use play money or your head. The reason why you can't do it on the calculator is because the calculator will cut the coin up in half.

Teacher comments:

This is an excellent explanation! How can this problem help you solve other problems? Can you think of a way to find the remainder using your calculator?

Mrs. Vasquez

Jayne's response the second day:

1. You can check your answer by the calculator you can put $1.66 + $1.66 + $1.66 + $0.02 = $5.00.

2. This problem can help me solve other problems because it will help me divide money (if it involves money.)

3. A way to find how much is left $5.00 – $1.66 – $1.66 – $1.66 = $0.02.

Figure 6: *Jayne's work*

Solving, 4

Jayne used both the play money and a calculator to divide the money efficiently. With a prompt from the teacher, she used two additional strategies to look back at her work and check her answer.

Knowing, 4

Jayne interpreted the problem as a division problem using both manipulatives and a calculator to perform the operation. All her calculations were accurate. Although unsophisticated, her first interpretation of the decimal she got when she used the calculator was almost correct when she said, ". . . the calculator will cut the coin up in half." With a hint from her teacher, she was able to use the calculator to include the remainder in her calculations by using repeated addition and then adding in the remainder. She was also able to connect this addition sentence to the corresponding number sentence using repeated subtraction.

Telling, 3

Jayne's responses were very clear, and she correctly used number sentences or words to explain each of her strategies. She discussed the answers she got on the calculator along with the answer she got using manipulatives. However, we do not know how the group shared the play money. Did they trade the dollars for quarters and then the quarters for dimes, etc., or were they able to make the process more efficient in some way?

Homework and Practice

- DPP Task L provides practice estimating sums. Bit M asks students to solve a mathhopper problem. Task N reviews finding the area of shapes.

- Home Practice Part 3 provides practice with estimating and measuring. Home Practice Part 4 provides practice with ordering fractions and solving problems involving fractions.

Answers for Parts 3 and 4 of the Home Practice are in the Answer Key at the end of this lesson and at the end of this unit.

Assessment

DPP Bit K is the *Multiplication Facts Inventory Test.*

Name _____ Date _____

PART 3

1. Four 8-gram masses, three 5-gram masses, and three 1-gram masses balance an object. What is the mass of the object?

2. **A.** Name something at home that is about 15 inches long.

   B. Name something that is about 15 cm long. _____

   C. Name something that is about one meter long. _____

3. A graduated cylinder is filled with water, six marbles of the same size are added, and the level of the water rises to 54 cc. Each marble has a volume of 4 cc. How much water is in the cylinder?

PART 4

1. Which number is the largest? Which is smallest? Explain how you know. $\frac{13}{10}$ 2/10   0.9

2. You are going to have a party. 1/2 of your guests will be relatives, 1/4 will be classmates, and 1/4 will be neighbors. Plan how many people you will invite. Draw a picture on paper and label it clearly.

3. **A.** At midnight on New Year's Eve, 50% of the 70 balloons at a party were popped by the guests. How many balloons were popped?

   B. Five children divided the rest of the balloons. How many balloons did each child get? _____

CONNECTIONS: AN ASSESSMENT UNIT   DAB • Grade 3 • Unit 20 **273**

Discovery Assignment Book - page 273 *(Answers on p. 63)*

Math Facts and Daily Practice and Problems

DPP Bit K is an inventory test on all the multiplication facts. Items L and M provide practice with addition and multiplication. Task N reviews area.

Teaching the Activity

1. Review student rubrics. Advise students that you will use the rubrics to score their work for this activity.
2. Students read the problems on the *Earning Money* Assessment Blackline Master and use play money, calculators, and student rubrics to solve them.
3. Students revise their work based on teacher comments.

Homework

Assign Home Practice Parts 3 and 4.

Assessment

1. DPP Bit K is the *Multiplication Facts Inventory Test*.
2. Score student work using the *TIMS Multidimensional Rubric*.

Answer Key is on pages 63–64.

Notes:

Name _____   Date _____

Earning Money

Daniel, Maria, and Cora earned five dollars baby-sitting for the Farleys. Mrs. Farley gave the three sitters one five-dollar bill.

1. If they share the money equally, how much should each baby-sitter get? Explain how you solved the problem.

2. What happens if you try to solve the problem on a calculator? Explain.

Write your solutions to Questions 1 and 2. Be sure to tell about all the ways you solved the problem.

More Money Masters

Blackline Master

More Money Masters

More Money Masters

Discovery Assignment Book (p. 273)

Home Practice*

Part 3

1. 50 grams

2. **A.** a newspaper, TV screen, placemat

   B. my mom's hand, a pencil, a stapler

   C. table top, height of a gym locker, the height of a chair

3. 30 cc

Part 4

1. $\frac{13}{10}$ is the largest; $\frac{2}{10}$ is the smallest. $\frac{13}{10}$ means I have more than one whole. $\frac{10}{10}$ is one whole. $\frac{2}{10}$ is part of a whole. $\frac{2}{10}$ is the same as 0.2. 0.9 is the same as $\frac{9}{10}$. 0.9 is almost a whole.

2. Answers will vary. 20 people; 10 will be relatives, 5 will be classmates, and 5 will be neighbors.

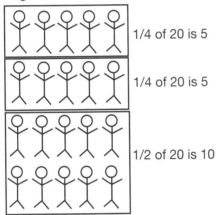

1/4 of 20 is 5

1/4 of 20 is 5

1/2 of 20 is 10

3. **A.** 35 balloons were popped.

   B. 7 balloons

Name _____ Date _____

PART 3

1. Four 8-gram masses, three 5-gram masses, and three 1-gram masses balance an object. What is the mass of the object?

2. **A.** Name something at home that is about 15 inches long.

   B. Name something that is about 15 cm long. _____

   C. Name something that is about one meter long. _____

3. A graduated cylinder is filled with water, six marbles of the same size are added, and the level of the water rises to 54 cc. Each marble has a volume of 4 cc. How much water is in the cylinder?

PART 4

1. Which number is the largest? Which is smallest? Explain how you know. $\frac{13}{10}$ 2/10   0.9

2. You are going to have a party. 1/2 of your guests will be relatives, 1/4 will be classmates, and 1/4 will be neighbors. Plan how many people you will invite. Draw a picture on paper and label it clearly.

3. **A.** At midnight on New Year's Eve, 50% of the 70 balloons at a party were popped by the guests. How many balloons were popped?

   B. Five children divided the rest of the balloons. How many balloons did each child get? _____

CONNECTIONS: AN ASSESSMENT UNIT   DAB • Grade 3 • Unit 20 **273**

Discovery Assignment Book - page 273

---

*Answers and/or discussion are included in the Lesson Guide.

Name _____ Date _____

Earning Money

Daniel, Maria, and Cora earned five dollars baby-sitting for the Farleys. Mrs. Farley gave the three sitters one five-dollar bill.

1. If they share the money equally, how much should each baby-sitter get? Explain how you solved the problem.

2. What happens if you try to solve the problem on a calculator? Explain.

Write your solutions to Questions 1 and 2. Be sure to tell about all the ways you solved the problem.

Assessment Blackline Master   URG • Grade 3 • Unit 20 • Lesson 4   **59**

Unit Resource Guide - **page 59**

Unit Resource Guide (p. 59)

Earning Money

See Figures 4–6 in the Lesson Guide for sample student work. Students' responses are graded using the *TIMS Multidimensional Rubric.**

*Answers and/or discussion are included in the Lesson Guide.

Lesson 5

End-of-Year Test

Lesson Overview

Students take a paper-and-pencil test consisting of 14 short items. Although these items test skills and concepts studied throughout the year, special emphasis is given to concepts addressed in the last ten units.

Key Content

• Assessing concepts and skills developed throughout the year.

Materials List

Supplies and Copies

Student	Teacher
Supplies for Each Student • centimeter ruler • calculator	**Supplies**
Copies • 1 copy of *End-of-Year Test* per student (*Unit Resource Guide* Pages 68–72)	**Copies/Transparencies**

All blackline masters including assessment, transparency, and DPP masters are also on the Teacher Resource CD.

Daily Practice and Problems and Home Practice

DPP items O–P (*Unit Resource Guide* Page 17)

Note: Classrooms whose pacing differs significantly from the suggested pacing of the units should use the Math Facts Calendar in Section 4 of the *Facts Resource Guide* to ensure students receive the complete math facts program.

Daily Practice and Problems

Suggestions for using the DPPs are below.

O. Bit: Play Digits: Sums (URG p. 17)

Draw boxes on your paper like these:

□ □ □
+ □ □
‾‾‾‾‾‾‾

As your teacher or classmate reads the digits, place them in the boxes. Try to find the highest sum. Remember, each digit will be read only once.

P. Task: Shaded Shapes (URG p. 17)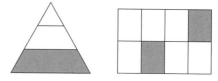

1. Is $\frac{1}{3}$ of the triangle shaded? Explain why or why not.
2. Is $\frac{1}{4}$ of the rectangle shaded? Explain why or why not.

Teaching the Activity

Students take the test individually. Although it was designed to take one class session to complete, you may wish to give students more time. Students will need centimeter rulers and should have access to calculators for the second part of the test. The first page of the test consists of an addition problem, a subtraction problem, and a multiplication problem. These problems assess students' fluency with multidigit addition, subtraction, and multiplication, so students should complete these items without the use of a calculator. Students should have the option of using a calculator for the remaining problems.

Emphasize the importance of following the directions for each item. Some items ask students to describe how they solved the problem. Encourage them to give full explanations of their problem-solving processes.

Homework and Practice

DPP item O develops addition number skills. Item P explores students' understanding of fraction concepts.

Assessment

Use the *End-of-Year Test* to assess students' skills and concepts studied throughout the year.

At a Glance

Math Facts and Daily Practice and Problems

DPP Bit O provides addition practice. Task P reviews fraction concepts.

Teaching the Activity

1. Students complete the first page of the test without a calculator.
2. Students complete the rest of the test with centimeter rulers and calculators.

Answer Key is on pages 73–75.

Notes:

End-of-Year Test

Part 1

You *may not* use your calculator on this page. You *may* use your calculator on the rest of the pages. Show how you solve each problem.

1. **A.** In one month, Mrs. Miranda's class read 7240 pages. During the same month, Mr. Carlton's class read 6965 pages. How many pages did both classes read?

   B. How many more pages did Mrs. Miranda's class read than Mr. Carlton's class?

2. Professor Peabody has to tile a hall. He will need five rows of tile, with 27 tiles in each row. How many tiles will he need?

Part 2

For the rest of the test, you may use any tools you used in class. For example, you may wish to use a ruler or a calculator.

3. Here is a shape to measure. Measure lengths to the nearest tenth of a centimeter.

   A. What is its area? _____

   B. What is its perimeter? _____

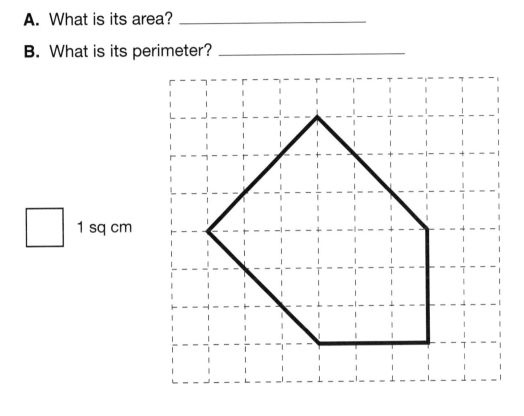

   1 sq cm

   C. How many sides does the shape have? _____

   D. How many vertices (corners) does it have? _____

   E. How many right angles does it have? _____

4. Daniel made 32 ounces of lemonade. How many 6-ounce cups could he fill? How much would be left over? Show your work.

5. Tell the time that is on the clock. _____

6. **A.** Write the coordinates of the triangle and square on the data table.

B. Draw the circle at the correct point on the map.

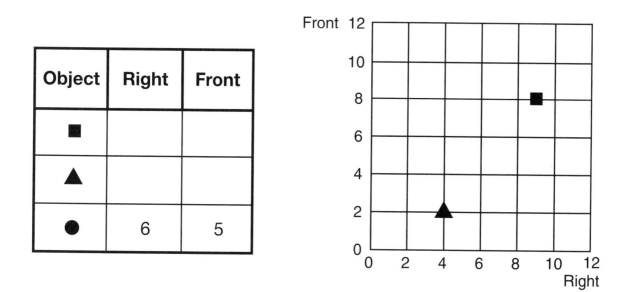

Object	Right	Front
■		
▲		
●	6	5

7. Show the number 2469 in base-ten shorthand.

8. A. Write $\frac{5}{10}$ as a decimal. _____

    B. Write 0.7 as a common fraction. _____

    C. Shade 0.5 of this picture.

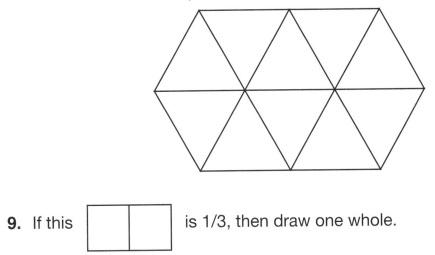

9. If this  is 1/3, then draw one whole.

10. Measure the length of the pencil to the nearest tenth of a centimeter.

    Length _____

11. Write three fractions that are equal to 1/2.

12. Which is bigger, 1.2 or $\frac{1}{2}$? Or are they equal? Tell how you know.

13. Dora put some marbles in one pan of a two-pan balance. She balanced the pans with three 10-gram masses, seven 5-gram masses, and two 1-gram masses. What is the marbles' mass? Explain how you found your answer.

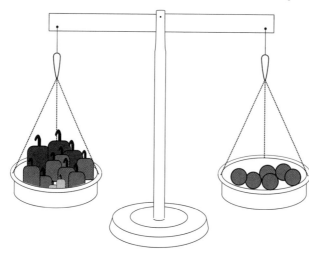

14. Peter put a rock in the water in the graduated cylinder shown below.

What was the volume of the rock? _____

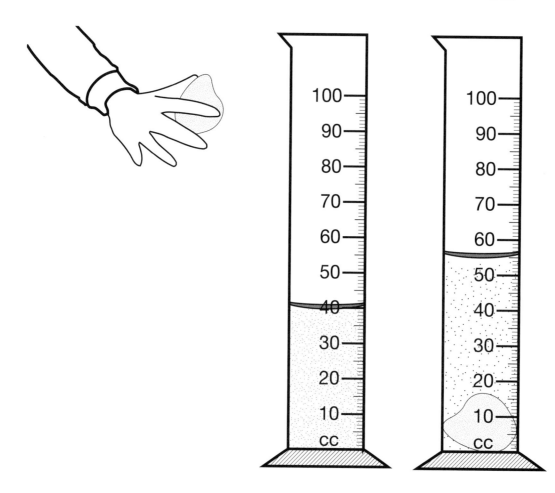

Copyright © Kendall/Hunt Publishing Company

Assessment Blackline Master

Unit Resource Guide (p. 68)

End-of-Year Test

I. **A.** 14,205 pages

   B. 275 pages

2. 135 tiles

Name _____ Date _____

End-of-Year Test

Part 1

You *may not* use your calculator on this page. You *may* use your calculator on the rest of the pages. Show how you solve each problem.

1. **A.** In one month, Mrs. Miranda's class read 7240 pages. During the same month, Mr. Carlton's class read 6965 pages. How many pages did both classes read?

   B. How many more pages did Mrs. Miranda's class read than Mr. Carlton's class?

2. Professor Peabody has to tile a hall. He will need five rows of tile, with 27 tiles in each row. How many tiles will he need?

68 URG • Grade 3 • Unit 20 • Lesson 5   Assessment Blackline Master

Unit Resource Guide - page 68

Unit Resource Guide (p. 69)

3. **A.** $22\frac{1}{2}$ square centimeters

   B. Measurements of each segment may be off by 0.1 cm. Accept any answer between 18.2–19.2 centimeters.

   C. 5 sides

   D. 5 vertices

   E. 3 right angles

4. 5 cups and 2 ounces remaining

Name _____ Date _____

Part 2

For the rest of the test, you may use any tools you used in class. For example, you may wish to use a ruler or a calculator.

3. Here is a shape to measure. Measure lengths to the nearest tenth of a centimeter.

   A. What is its area? _____

   B. What is its perimeter? _____

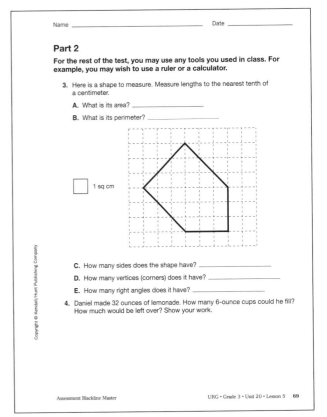

1 sq cm

   C. How many sides does the shape have? _____

   D. How many vertices (corners) does it have? _____

   E. How many right angles does it have? _____

4. Daniel made 32 ounces of lemonade. How many 6-ounce cups could he fill? How much would be left over? Show your work.

Assessment Blackline Master   URG • Grade 3 • Unit 20 • Lesson 5 **69**

Unit Resource Guide - page 69

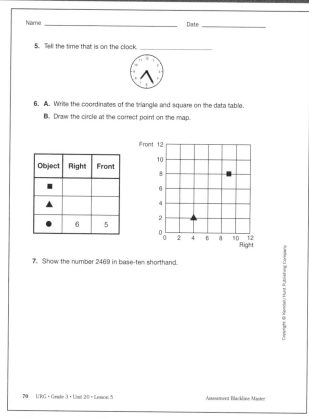

Name _____ Date _____

5. Tell the time that is on the clock. _____

6. **A.** Write the coordinates of the triangle and square on the data table.

   B. Draw the circle at the correct point on the map.

Object	Right	Front
■		
▲		
●	6	5

7. Show the number 2469 in base-ten shorthand.

Unit Resource Guide - page 70

Unit Resource Guide (p. 70)

5. 7:25

6. **A.** square: 9 right, 8 front
   triangle: 4 right, 2 front

   B. The dot should be placed at 6 right, 5 front.

7.

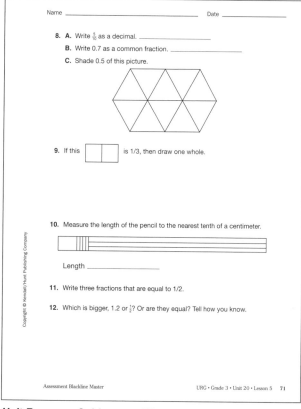

Name _____ Date _____

8. **A.** Write $\frac{5}{10}$ as a decimal. _____
   B. Write 0.7 as a common fraction. _____
   C. Shade 0.5 of this picture.

9. If this [|] is 1/3, then draw one whole.

10. Measure the length of the pencil to the nearest tenth of a centimeter.

   Length _____

11. Write three fractions that are equal to 1/2.

12. Which is bigger, 1.2 or ½? Or are they equal? Tell how you know.

Unit Resource Guide - page 71

Unit Resource Guide (p. 71)

8. **A.** 0.5
   B. $\frac{7}{10}$
   C. Any five triangles can be shaded.

9. Shapes will vary. Here are three examples.

10. 14.7–14.9 centimeters

11. Answers will vary. Possible answers are:
    2/4, 7/14, and 50/100

12. 1.2 is larger; 1.2 is larger than one whole. 1/2 is part of a whole or less than one whole.

Unit Resource Guide (p. 72)

13. 67 grams; explanations will vary. 3×10 grams $+ 7 \times 5$ grams $+ 2 \times 1$ gram $= 67$ grams

14. 15 cc; 55 cc $-$ 40 cc $=$ 15 cc

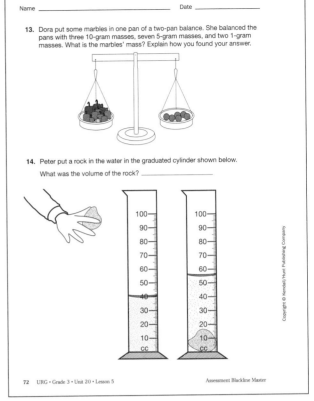

Name _____ Date _____

13. Dora put some marbles in one pan of a two-pan balance. She balanced the pans with three 10-gram masses, seven 5-gram masses, and two 1-gram masses. What is the marbles' mass? Explain how you found your answer.

14. Peter put a rock in the water in the graduated cylinder shown below. What was the volume of the rock? _____

72   URG • Grade 3 • Unit 20 • Lesson 5   Assessment Blackline Master

Unit Resource Guide - page 72

Name _____ Date _____

Unit 20 Home Practice

PART 1

1.
$$\begin{array}{r} 70 \\ \times\ 9 \\ \hline \end{array}$$

2.
$$\begin{array}{r} 877 \\ +\ 549 \\ \hline \end{array}$$

3.
$$\begin{array}{r} 51 \\ \times\ 8 \\ \hline \end{array}$$

4.
$$\begin{array}{r} 551 \\ -\ 435 \\ \hline \end{array}$$

5. $400 - 237 =$ _____   6. $719 + 281 =$ _____   7. $46 \times 3 =$ _____

8. In the morning, Alex spends 25 minutes getting ready for school, an hour delivering papers, and 15 minutes walking to school. If Alex must be at school by 8:00, what time should he wake up?

Show your work. _____

PART 2

1.
$$\begin{array}{r} 893 \\ -\ 5 \\ \hline \end{array}$$

2.
$$\begin{array}{r} 893 \\ -\ 95 \\ \hline \end{array}$$

3.
$$\begin{array}{r} 893 \\ -\ 495 \\ \hline \end{array}$$

4.
$$\begin{array}{r} 645 \\ +\ 6 \\ \hline \end{array}$$

5.
$$\begin{array}{r} 645 \\ +\ 86 \\ \hline \end{array}$$

6.
$$\begin{array}{r} 645 \\ +\ 986 \\ \hline \end{array}$$

7. Explain a strategy for solving Question 2 in your head.

8. A. At the movies, Roberto's mom spent $5.75 on two drinks and one bag of popcorn. If each drink costs $1.75, how much did the popcorn cost?

B. If she paid with a ten-dollar bill, how much change should Roberto's mom get back?

272 DAB • Grade 3 • Unit 20   CONNECTIONS: AN ASSESSMENT UNIT

Discovery Assignment Book - page 272

Discovery Assignment Book (p. 272)

Part 1

1. 630
2. 1426
3. 408
4. 116
5. 163
6. 1000
7. 138
8. 6:20 A.M.

Part 2

1. 888
2. 798
3. 398
4. 651
5. 731
6. 1631
7. Possible strategy: $893 - 100 = 793$
   $793 + 5 = 798$
8. A. $2.25
   B. $4.25

*Answers and/or discussion are included in the Lesson Guide.

Discovery Assignment Book (p. 273)

Part 3

1. 50 grams

2. **A.** a newspaper, TV screen, placemat

   B. my mom's hand, a pencil, a stapler

   C. table top, height of a gym locker, the height of a chair

3. 30 cc

Part 4

1. $\frac{13}{10}$ is the largest; $\frac{2}{10}$ is the smallest. $\frac{13}{10}$ means I have more than one whole. $\frac{10}{10}$ is one whole. $\frac{2}{10}$ is part of a whole. $\frac{2}{10}$ is the same as 0.2. 0.9 is the same as $\frac{9}{10}$. 0.9 is almost a whole.

2. Answers will vary. 20 people; 10 will be relatives, 5 will be classmates, and 5 will be neighbors.

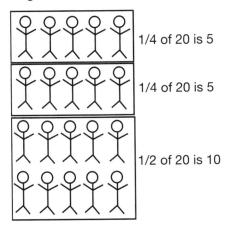

1/4 of 20 is 5

1/4 of 20 is 5

1/2 of 20 is 10

3. **A.** 35 balloons were popped.

   B. 7 balloons

Name _____ Date _____

PART 3

1. Four 8-gram masses, three 5-gram masses, and three 1-gram masses balance an object. What is the mass of the object?
_____

2. **A.** Name something at home that is about 15 inches long.
_____

   B. Name something that is about 15 cm long. _____

   C. Name something that is about one meter long. _____

3. A graduated cylinder is filled with water, six marbles of the same size are added, and the level of the water rises to 54 cc. Each marble has a volume of 4 cc. How much water is in the cylinder?
_____

PART 4

1. Which number is the largest? Which is smallest? Explain how you know. $\frac{13}{10}$ 2/10   0.9

2. You are going to have a party. 1/2 of your guests will be relatives, 1/4 will be classmates, and 1/4 will be neighbors. Plan how many people you will invite. Draw a picture on paper and label it clearly.

3. **A.** At midnight on New Year's Eve, 50% of the 70 balloons at a party were popped by the guests. How many balloons were popped?
_____

   B. Five children divided the rest of the balloons. How many balloons did each child get? _____

CONNECTIONS: AN ASSESSMENT UNIT   DAB • Grade 3 • Unit 20 **273**

Discovery Assignment Book - page 273

---

*Answers and/or discussion are included in the Lesson Guide.

Glossary

This glossary provides definitions of key vocabulary terms in the Grade 3 lessons. Locations of key vocabulary terms in the curriculum are included with each definition. Components Key: URG = *Unit Resource Guide*, SG = *Student Guide*, and DAB = *Discovery Assignment Book*.

A

Area (URG Unit 5; SG Unit 5)
The area of a shape is the amount of space it covers, measured in square units.

Array (URG Unit 7 & Unit 11)
An array is an arrangement of elements into a rectangular pattern of (horizontal) rows and (vertical) columns. (*See* column and row.)

Associative Property of Addition (URG Unit 2)
For any three numbers a, b, and c we have $a + (b + c) = (a + b) + c$. For example in finding the sum of 4, 8, and 2, one can compute $4 + 8$ first and then add 2: $(4 + 8) + 2 = 14$. Alternatively, we can compute $8 + 2$ and then add the result to 4: $4 + (8 + 2) = 4 + 10 = 14$.

Average (URG Unit 5)
A number that can be used to represent a typical value in a set of data. (*See also* mean and median.)

Axes (URG Unit 8; SG Unit 8)
Reference lines on a graph. In the Cartesian coordinate system, the axes are two perpendicular lines that meet at the origin. The singular of axes is axis.

B

Base (of a cube model) (URG Unit 18; SG Unit 18)
The part of a cube model that sits on the "ground."

Base-Ten Board (URG Unit 4)
A tool to help children organize base-ten pieces when they are representing numbers.

Base-Ten Pieces (URG Unit 4; SG Unit 4)
A set of manipulatives used to model our number system as shown in the figure at the right. Note that a skinny is made of 10 bits, a flat is made of 100 bits, and a pack is made of 1000 bits.

Base-Ten Shorthand (SG Unit 4)
A pictorial representation of the base-ten pieces as shown.

Nickname	Picture	Shorthand
bit		·
skinny		/
flat		
pack		

Best-Fit Line (URG Unit 9; SG Unit 9; DAB Unit 9)
The line that comes closest to the most number of points on a point graph.

Bit (URG Unit 4; SG Unit 4)
A cube that measures 1 cm on each edge. It is the smallest of the base-ten pieces that is often used to represent 1. (*See also* base-ten pieces.)

C

Capacity (URG Unit 16)
1. The volume of the inside of a container.
2. The largest volume a container can hold.

Cartesian Coordinate System (URG Unit 8)
A method of locating points on a flat surface by means of numbers. This method is named after its originator, René Descartes. (*See also* coordinates.)

Centimeter (cm)
A unit of measure in the metric system equal to one-hundredth of a meter. (1 inch = 2.54 cm)

Column (URG Unit 11)
In an array, the objects lined up vertically.

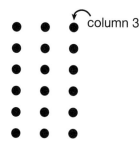
column 3

Common Fraction (URG Unit 15)
Any fraction that is written with a numerator and denominator that are whole numbers. For example, $\frac{3}{4}$ and $\frac{9}{4}$ are both common fractions. (*See also* decimal fraction.)

Commutative Property of Addition (URG Unit 2 & Unit 11)
This is also known as the Order Property of Addition. Changing the order of the addends does not change the sum. For example, $3 + 5 = 5 + 3 = 8$. Using variables, $n + m = m + n$.

Commutative Property of Multiplication (URG Unit 11)
Changing the order of the factors in a multiplication problem does not change the result, e.g., $7 \times 3 = 3 \times 7 = 21$. (*See also* turn-around facts.)

Congruent (URG Unit 12 & Unit 17; SG Unit 12)
Figures with the same shape and size.

Convenient Number (URG Unit 6)
A number used in computation that is close enough to give a good estimate, but is also easy to compute mentally, e.g., 25 and 30 are convenient numbers for 27.

Coordinates (URG Unit 8; SG Unit 8)
An ordered pair of numbers that locates points on a flat surface by giving distances from a pair of coordinate axes. For example, if a point has coordinates (4, 5) it is 4 units from the vertical axis and 5 units from the horizontal axis.

Counting Back (URG Unit 2)
A strategy for subtracting in which students start from a larger number and then count down until the number is reached. For example, to solve $8 - 3$, begin with 8 and count down three, 7, 6, 5.

Counting Down (*See* counting back.)

Counting Up (URG Unit 2)
A strategy for subtraction in which the student starts at the lower number and counts on to the higher number. For example, to solve $8 - 5$, the student starts at 5 and counts up three numbers (6, 7, 8). So $8 - 5 = 3$.

Cube (SG Unit 18)
A three-dimensional shape with six congruent square faces.

Cubic Centimeter (cc) (URG Unit 16; SG Unit 16)
The volume of a cube that is one centimeter long on each edge.

1 cm
1 cm
1 cm
cubic centimeter

Cup (URG Unit 16)
A unit of volume equal to 8 fluid ounces, one-half pint.

D

Decimal Fraction (URG Unit 15)
A fraction written as a decimal. For example, 0.75 and 0.4 are decimal fractions and $\frac{75}{100}$ and $\frac{4}{10}$ are called common fractions. (*See also* fraction.)

Denominator (URG Unit 13)
The number below the line in a fraction. The denominator indicates the number of equal parts in which the unit whole is divided. For example, the 5 is the denominator in the fraction $\frac{2}{5}$. In this case the unit whole is divided into five equal parts.

Density (URG Unit 16)
The ratio of an object's mass to its volume.

Difference (URG Unit 2)
The answer to a subtraction problem.

Dissection (URG Unit 12 & Unit 17)
Cutting or decomposing a geometric shape into smaller shapes that cover it exactly.

Distributive Property of Multiplication over Addition (URG Unit 19)
For any three numbers a, b, and c, $a \times (b + c) = a \times b + a \times c$. The distributive property is the foundation for most methods of multidigit multiplication. For example, $9 \times (17) = 9 \times (10 + 7) = 9 \times 10 + 9 \times 7 = 90 + 63 = 153$.

E

Equal-Arm Balance
See two-pan balance.

Equilateral Triangle (URG Unit 7)
A triangle with all sides of equal length and all angles of equal measure.

Equivalent Fractions (SG Unit 17)
Fractions that have the same value, e.g., $\frac{2}{4} = \frac{1}{2}$.

Estimate (URG Unit 5 & Unit 6)
1. (verb) To find *about* how many.
2. (noun) An approximate number.

Extrapolation (URG Unit 7)
Using patterns in data to make predictions or to estimate values that lie beyond the range of values in the set of data.

F

Fact Family (URG Unit 11; SG Unit 11)
Related math facts, e.g., $3 \times 4 = 12$, $4 \times 3 = 12$, $12 \div 3 = 4$, $12 \div 4 = 3$.

Factor (URG Unit 11; SG Unit 11)
1. In a multiplication problem, the numbers that are multiplied together. In the problem $3 \times 4 = 12$, 3 and 4 are the factors.
2. Whole numbers that can be multiplied together to get a number. That is, numbers that divide a number evenly, e.g., 1, 2, 3, 4, 6, and 12 are all the factors of 12.

Fewest Pieces Rule (URG Unit 4 & Unit 6; SG Unit 4)
Using the least number of base-ten pieces to represent a number. (*See also* base-ten pieces.)

Flat (URG Unit 4; SG Unit 4)
A block that measures 1 cm × 10 cm × 10 cm. It is one of the base-ten pieces that is often used to represent 100. (*See also* base-ten pieces.)

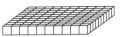

Flip (URG Unit 12)
A motion of the plane in which a figure is reflected over a line so that any point and its image are the same distance from the line.

Fraction (URG Unit 15)
A number that can be written as $\frac{a}{b}$ where a and b are whole numbers and b is not zero. For example, $\frac{1}{2}$, 0.5, and 2 are all fractions since 0.5 can be written as $\frac{5}{10}$ and 2 can be written as $\frac{2}{1}$.

Front-End Estimation (URG Unit 6)
Estimation by looking at the left-most digit.

G

Gallon (gal) (URG Unit 16)
A unit of volume equal to four quarts.

Gram
The basic unit used to measure mass.

H

Hexagon (SG Unit 12)
A six-sided polygon.

Horizontal Axis (SG Unit 1)
In a coordinate grid, the *x*-axis. The axis that extends from left to right.

I

Interpolation (URG Unit 7)
Making predictions or estimating values that lie between data points in a set of data.

J

K

Kilogram
1000 grams.

L

Likely Event (SG Unit 1)
An event that has a high probability of occurring.

Line of Symmetry (URG Unit 12)
A line is a line of symmetry for a plane figure if, when the figure is folded along this line, the two parts match exactly.

Line Symmetry (URG Unit 12; SG Unit 12)
A figure has line symmetry if it has at least one line of symmetry.

Liter (l) (URG Unit 16; SG Unit 16)
Metric unit used to measure volume. A liter is a little more than a quart.

M

Magic Square (URG Unit 2)
A square array of digits in which the sums of the rows, columns, and main diagonals are the same.

Making a Ten (URG Unit 2)
Strategies for addition and subtraction that make use of knowing the sums to ten. For example, knowing $6 + 4 = 10$ can be helpful in finding $10 - 6 = 4$ and $11 - 6 = 5$.

Mass (URG Unit 9 & Unit 16; SG Unit 9)
The amount of matter in an object.

Mean (URG Unit 5)
An average of a set of numbers that is found by adding the values of the data and dividing by the number of values.

Measurement Division (URG Unit 7)
Division as equal grouping. The total number of objects and the number of objects in each group are known. The number of groups is the unknown. For example, tulip bulbs come in packages of 8. If 216 bulbs are sold, how many packages are sold?

Measurement Error (URG Unit 9)
The unavoidable error that occurs due to the limitations inherent to any measurement instrument.

Median (URG Unit 5; DAB Unit 5)
For a set with an odd number of data arranged in order, it is the middle number. For an even number of data arranged in order, it is the number halfway between the two middle numbers.

Meniscus (URG Unit 16; SG Unit 16)
The curved surface formed when a liquid creeps up the side of a container (for example, a graduated cylinder).

Meter (m)
The standard unit of length measure in the metric system. One meter is approximately 39 inches.

Milliliter (ml) (URG Unit 16; SG Unit 16)
A measure of capacity in the metric system that is the volume of a cube that is one centimeter long on each edge.

Multiple (URG Unit 3 & Unit 11)
A number is a multiple of another number if it is evenly divisible by that number. For example, 12 is a multiple of 2 since 2 divides 12 evenly.

N

Numerator (URG Unit 13)
The number written above the line in a fraction. For example, the 2 is the numerator in the fraction $\frac{2}{5}$.
(*See also* denominator.)

O

One-Dimensional Object (URG Unit 18; SG Unit 18)
An object is one-dimensional if it is made up of pieces of lines and curves.

Ordered Pairs (URG Unit 8)
A pair of numbers that gives the coordinates of a point on a grid in relation to the origin. The horizontal coordinate is given first; the vertical coordinate is given second. For example, the ordered pair (5, 3) tells us to move five units to the right of the origin and 3 units up.

Origin (URG Unit 8)
The point at which the x- and y-axes (horizontal and vertical axes) intersect on a coordinate plane. The origin is described by the ordered pair (0, 0) and serves as a reference point so that all the points on the plane can be located by ordered pairs.

P

Pack (URG Unit 4; SG Unit 4)
A cube that measures 10 cm on each edge. It is one of the base-ten pieces that is often used to represent 1000.
(*See also* base-ten pieces.)

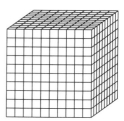

Palindrome (URG Unit 6)
A number, word, or phrase that reads the same forward and backward, e.g., 12321.

Parallel Lines (URG Unit 18)
Lines that are in the same direction. In the plane, parallel lines are lines that do not intersect.

Parallelogram (URG Unit 18)
A quadrilateral with two pairs of parallel sides.

Partitive Division (URG Unit 7)
Division as equal sharing. The total number of objects and the number of groups are known. The number of objects in each group is the unknown. For example, Frank has 144 marbles that he divides equally into 6 groups. How many marbles are in each group?

Pentagon (SG Unit 12)
A five-sided, five-angled polygon.

Perimeter (URG Unit 7; DAB Unit 7)
The distance around a two-dimensional shape.

Pint (URG Unit 16)
A unit of volume measure equal to 16 fluid ounces, i.e., two cups.

Polygon
A two-dimensional connected figure made of line segments in which each endpoint of every side meets with an endpoint of exactly one other side.

Population (URG Unit 1; SG Unit 1)
A collection of persons or things whose properties will be analyzed in a survey or experiment.

Prediction (SG Unit 1)
Using data to declare or foretell what is likely to occur.

Prime Number (URG Unit 11)
A number that has exactly two factors. For example, 7 has exactly two distinct factors, 1 and 7.

Prism
A three-dimensional figure that has two congruent faces, called bases, that are parallel to each other, and all other faces are parallelograms.

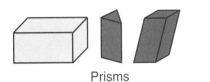

Prisms   Not a prism

Product (URG Unit 11; SG Unit 11; DAB Unit 11)
The answer to a multiplication problem. In the problem $3 \times 4 = 12$, 12 is the product.

Q

Quadrilateral (URG Unit 18)
A polygon with four sides.

Quart (URG Unit 16)
A unit of volume equal to 32 fluid ounces; one quarter of a gallon.

R

Recording Sheet (URG Unit 4)
A place value chart used for addition and subtraction problems.

Rectangular Prism (URG Unit 18; SG Unit 18)
A prism whose bases are rectangles. A right rectangular prism is a prism having all faces rectangles.

Regular (URG Unit 7; DAB Unit 7)
A polygon is regular if all sides are of equal length and all angles are equal.

Remainder (URG Unit 7)
Something that remains or is left after a division problem. The portion of the dividend that is not evenly divisible by the divisor, e.g., $16 \div 5 = 3$ with 1 as a remainder.

Right Angle (SG Unit 12)
An angle that measures 90°.

Rotation (turn) (URG Unit 12)
A transformation (motion) in which a figure is turned a specified angle and direction around a point.

Row (URG Unit 11)
In an array, the objects lined up horizontally.

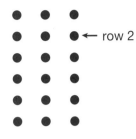

Rubric (URG Unit 2)
A written guideline for assigning scores to student work, for the purpose of assessment.

S

Sample (URG Unit 1; SG Unit 1)
A part or subset of a population.

Skinny (URG Unit 4; SG Unit 4)
A block that measures 1 cm $\times$ 1 cm $\times$ 10 cm. It is one of the base-ten pieces that is often used to represent 10. (*See also* base-ten pieces.)

Square Centimeter (sq cm) (SG Unit 5)
The area of a square that is 1 cm long on each side.

Square Number (SG Unit 11)
A number that is the product of a whole number multiplied by itself. For example, 25 is a square number since $5 \times 5 = 25$. A square number can be represented by a square array with the same number of rows as columns. A square array for 25 has 5 rows of 5 objects in each row or 25 total objects.

Standard Masses
A set of objects with convenient masses, usually 1 g, 10 g, 100 g, etc.

Sum (URG Unit 2; SG Unit 2)
The answer to an addition problem.

Survey (URG Unit 14; SG Unit 14)
An investigation conducted by collecting data from a sample of a population and then analyzing it. Usually surveys are used to make predictions about the entire population.

T

Tangrams (SG Unit 12)
A type of geometric puzzle. A shape is given and it must be covered exactly with seven standard shapes called tans.

Thinking Addition (URG Unit 2)
A strategy for subtraction that uses a related addition problem. For example, $15 - 7 = 8$ because $8 + 7 = 15$.

Three-Dimensional (URG Unit 18; SG Unit 18)
Existing in three-dimensional space; having length, width, and depth.

TIMS Laboratory Method (URG Unit 1; SG Unit 1)
A method that students use to organize experiments and investigations. It involves four components: draw, collect, graph, and explore. It is a way to help students learn about the scientific method.

Turn (URG Unit 12)
(*See* rotation.)

Turn-Around Facts (URG Unit 2 & Unit 11 p. 37; SG Unit 11)
Addition facts that have the same addends but in a different order, e.g., $3 + 4 = 7$ and $4 + 3 = 7$. (*See also* commutative property of addition and commutative property of multiplication.)

Two-Dimensional (URG Unit 18; SG Unit 18)
Existing in the plane; having length and width.

Two-Pan Balance
A device for measuring the mass of an object by balancing the object against a number of standard masses (usually multiples of 1 unit, 10 units, and 100 units, etc.).

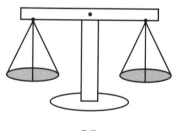

U

Unit (of measurement) (URG Unit 18)
A precisely fixed quantity used to measure. For example, centimeter, foot, kilogram, and quart are units of measurement.

Using a Ten (URG Unit 2)
1. A strategy for addition that uses partitions of the number 10. For example, one can find $8 + 6$ by thinking $8 + 6 = 8 + 2 + 4 = 10 + 4 = 14$.
2. A strategy for subtraction that uses facts that involve subtracting 10. For example, students can use $17 - 10 = 7$ to learn the "close fact" $17 - 9 = 8$.

Using Doubles (URG Unit 2)
Strategies for addition and subtraction that use knowing doubles. For example, one can find $7 + 8$ by thinking $7 + 8 = 7 + 7 + 1 = 14 + 1 = 15$. Knowing $7 + 7 = 14$ can be helpful in finding $14 - 7 = 7$ and $14 - 8 = 6$.

V

Value (URG Unit 1; SG Unit 1)
The possible outcomes of a variable. For example, red, green, and blue are possible values for the variable *color*. Two meters and 1.65 meters are possible values for the variable *length*.

Variable (URG Unit 1; SG Unit 1)
1. An attribute or quantity that changes or varies.
2. A symbol that can stand for a variable.

Vertex (URG Unit 12; SG Unit 12)
1. A point where the sides of a polygon meet.
2. A point where the edges of a three-dimensional object meet.

Vertical Axis (SG Unit 1)
In a coordinate grid, the *y*-axis. It is perpendicular to the horizontal axis.

Volume (URG Unit 16; SG Unit 16)
The measure of the amount of space occupied by an object.

Volume by Displacement (URG Unit 16)
A way of measuring volume of an object by measuring the amount of water (or some other fluid) it displaces.

W

Weight (URG Unit 9)
A measure of the pull of gravity on an object. One unit for measuring weight is the pound.

X

Y

Z